The Seventh Sense

The Seventh Sense

The Key to Effectiveness in Life and Business

Brendan J. Cunningham

Outskirts Press, Inc.
Denver, Colorado

The Seventh Sense
The Key to Effectiveness in Life and Business

Outskirts Press, Inc.
http://www.outskirtspress.com

ISBN: 978-1-4327-6119-6

Library of Congress Control Number: 2010930389

Outskirts Press and the "OP" logo are trademarks belonging to Outskirts Press, Inc.

PRINTED IN THE UNITED STATES OF AMERICA

To Kathleen who continues to inspire me and never ceases to astonish me.

Contents

Acknowledgements

It is with deep gratitude that I acknowledge all of the following for their contributions in helping me shape my thoughts and giving me the guidance and or encouragement that helped me create this book.

To two of my partners Joni Stovroff and Jacque Taylor who run two of the most successful businesses in Western New York and who continue to inspire me and who define the power of the Seventh Sense. This is especially true of Joni who at age 77 was recognized in Business First Magazine as being the Business Person of the year. And let's be real clear about something. One does not get that accolade for popularity or for being around for a long time. You earn it by being at the top of your game. Anyone that knows her will tell you she's a pistol. She could tell Donald Trump,

"You're fired."

To Rachel Suminski, who I humorously refer to as "the girl you love to hate." I say this because she is not only good at what she does, but she is kind hearted, generous and when you throw in beautiful, it makes some of her peers just want to drop a safe on her head. She is a young entrepreneur who I have had the pleasure to observe and work with and whose Seventh Sense seems to almost exude from her pores. When I see people like her (which is not often), I gain a greater sense of relief that the world of tomorrow will truly be in the hands of well deserved, right thinking, leadership. Her continued successes remind me that the Seventh Sense is alive and well in the next generation. They will need it.

To Alice Cunningham whose insights provided me with a series of different perspectives in making this a better book and whose editing helped make the entire work an easier read. She is a gifted and emerging leader whose Seventh Sense is only beginning to unleash itself. Her efforts together with my friends at Outskirts Press, especially Tinamarie Ruvalcaba, helped produce a book that hopefully my readers will enjoy and recommend.

To Jean Seibert, my former mother-in-law, I extend my gratitude as well. At 94 years of age she continues to look beautiful inside and out. I still enjoy making her blush when I describe her to my friends, upon introduction, as a "hot tuna." But my reason for including her here is not so much because of my affection for her but for my recognition of her Seventh Sense. It has served her well. Her ability to get things done in the lady like way she always manages to do so is glorious.

And a special salute to Liz Vogel for a super cool cover design. It captured the essence of the Seventh Sense in ways that I hoped it would. She is a special talent indeed and a young lady whose own Seventh Sense will take her far.

You may have noticed that all of the acknowledgments to this point are to women. If you have, than you are inordinately perceptive. It isn't an accident. As you read this book, you will begin to understand not only what the Seventh Sense is but how it can help you get better control of your life and business. You will also come to realize that this is a power that is more abundant in women than it is in men. This might be something that has just become a natural part of our DNA which has evolved over the millennia or co-incidence. Either way, few will argue that it is the women of the world that seem to push the envelope and get things done. This is true for both themselves and their families. It may sound sexist to some but I have to say there is a relentless amount of truth to the axiom that "behind every great man, there is a great woman." Women are the unsung heroes throughout history and I am happy to say that the glass ceiling is cracking in some places and shattered in others. It is truly an idea whose time has come.

One man, however, is owed an "homage": Dr. John Frederick. I would be seriously remiss if I did not mention his contribution to me both personally and professionally. In spite of his casual demeanor, I was never comfortable addressing him as John but as my professor at Daemen College, he brought me to a newer realization of the complexities of Leadership. My studies with him and his tutelage have been pivotal in the development of many of the concepts that have gone into the making of this book. To all of the above, I extend my sincerest thanks.

Introduction

Before we get too far, let me give you some background on who I am, what you will be reading in this book, and what my qualifications are to speak on this subject at all. Let's think about the title and let me ask you this first question. Have you ever gone to a seminar or picked up a motivational book and gotten yourself all pumped up and felt like "Yeah, now I can go out and do anything." Those feeling are great, and all of that is certainly well and good, and I am not going to tell you to not do that anymore, but I am going to question the long-term effectiveness of it.

Frequently one leaves these seminars and much like Luke Skywalker, they almost seem to *feel the force*. Sadly though this lasts for about 20 minutes, and then it is business as usual right afterwards. In essence, nothing really happens. Many years ago when I first started to develop my prowess as a motivational speaker, my mentor at the time, Dave Kovalsky, would tell me, "if you speak to them and it doesn't change their behavior it is a waste of time." That was pretty harsh sounding at the time, but I have to admit, it was just as right on point then as it is now. So over the years I have worked to become not so much a *Motivational* speaker but one that is closer to what I describe as a ***pre--motivational*** speaker. What's that, you say? (Actually you probably asked that after you said, "Yikes, where the hell is this guy going with this?")

My response when I am asked about this is something that stems from what I learned in my days as a sales manager running large Real Estate offices and has developed as an extension of this. Here is what I would tell ALL the agents that ever worked for me, before I even hired them. **"I will never tell you what you want to hear; I will tell you what you need to know."** Now I would make every effort not to hurt their feelings and would always try to work with them so they could save face. But what was the point in lying to them? Was there any benefit in giving them false hope? How would I live with myself if I did? Should I have, in effect, bundled them in a blanket of deceit in an effort to protect them from what was really going on in their respective businesses? No way.

I am not going to tell you that this is not Standard Operating Procedures for many sales managers in a host of different industries. It just wasn't going to happen on my watch and it didn't, and as a result I earned a reputation as a straight shooter, one who you could trust and one that would help you get to the next level if you were willing to do what I told you to do. Guess what? I still do this. In the pages ahead I promise you I am not going to tell you what you want to hear. I will tell you what you need to know and I will do it in a way that sometimes might even make you laugh. That's ok too. But I want you to GET IT. As for the notion of my being a pre-motivational speaker, let me say this. I think before soil can produce any kind of vegetative growth, it has to be fertile. My job is to add the proper amount of humus and nutrients to the soil. Before someone is motivated to change they have to be ready. I get them ready to hear what they need to hear so they can go on to do what they need to do.

When I am not going around the country speaking on various subjects, from Leadership, to sales management, from team building to customer service, I am a business consultant and coach. I run a company called Excelleron Business Consulting, which is based out of Western New York in a town called Hamburg. Through my company, I am personally and professionally dedicated to getting my clients to the next level. I work with them to build them to the point where they can begin "working on" their respective businesses rather than "in" them. The companies I work with range from employing as few as 1 to up to 952. Succinctly put, I take frustrated entrepreneurs and turn them into focused and successful business people. And guess what, it isn't easy. Nothing that is truly worthwhile ever is, but I would be remiss if I didn't tell you that I find my work incredibly enjoyable and extremely rewarding both personally and financially. I am also a principal in a Real Estate company called Stovroff & Taylor Realtors which just made the Business First list of top 50 fastest growing companies in the region known as Western New York in 2009. It was also recognized as one of the best places to work as well. Coincidence: you be the judge?

Let me give you a little more background on who I am and how the basis of this book came into being. Many years ago while traveling through Northern Spain, I learned a saying. "Life was a chain." So I quess the first link in that chain for me was starting out as a working actor on the New York stage with a bit of moonlighting in soaps and commercials. That experience would serve me well in years to come before I would begin to learn my craft in the Real Estate business.

Later I went on to consult with Fortune 500 companies and my expertise would grow and take me to an international audience. To date I have done well over 1500 speaking engagements. As a proud member of the press, I have written books and a myriad of articles. Currently I produce two newsletters a month and generally do what I can do to get the word out and make the world a better place. Now I know this last parts sounds pretty **high falooting**, but like Stephen Covey recommends, I like "to begin with the end in mind." The "end in mind" is to tell you what you need to know. If you begin to get a sense of this there is a much higher probability that you might just possibly act on whatever it is that you have just had your epiphany on and you will in fact: "act on it." If everyone simply did what they needed to do or wanted to do in a methodical fashion we would have real progress and the world would indeed be a better place. That makes sense, doesn't it?

So I won't tell you what you want to hear. If you are up to it, and I hope that you are, than read on with an open mind. If you were hoping to pick up another book with useless but nice sounding platitudes, ok; I will give you some, but not without my own editorial comments because I am not here to make you simply feel good. If that is what you want, put the book down and go and have a glass of wine and put your feet up by the fireplace. Hell, that's what I do and that works pretty well for me. But if you want to be bothered a little and have your thoughts provoked, if you want to be shaken so that you can "get on" or "back on track", if you want to get to the next level in your life, than I am your man and this is the book that you need to be reading and to paraphrase four-time super bowl coach Marv Levy, you need to be reading it "right here, right now." I don't think there are any accidents in life and this is another example of that belief. It is no accident that you have chosen to pick up this book. It is written to be an easy read but the concepts are designed to be emotionally and intellectually challenging.

In some instances you may find what I have to say, "paradigm shifting." Either way, it's all good if it effects a change in you. My mission is to have you achieve measurable change. So keep an open mind. Determine for yourself initially what it is you want to get done, accomplished or achieved and begin reading chapter 1. I ask you to do this; because you will actually write it down before too long but for now just begin to create it in your own mind.

This is your first exercise. Visualize what it is that you want. Ask yourself

- What will it be like when you have it?
- When do you hope to have it or achieve it? You should have two different time frames for this one. When would you like to have it and when must you have it absolutely?
- Why do you want it? If you say I need more money what would you do with it?
- How do you go about starting the process to get it?
- Where will you be when you get it?
- Whose help will you need along the way? No one, as you soon will learn, gets up the mountain by themselves.

If you surrender to this first exercise you will be further along then most and ultimately you will be well on your way to harnessing the power of your **Seventh Sense**. Later as you hewn this power which all of us possess to one degree or another, you will get the EDG which is an acronym for Effortless Directional Growth.

If you possess the faculty at all you should be developing a sense of uneasiness already. You should find yourself restless thinking that you would like to know more about this power. Suffice it to say that we will get you there in time and fully expand on how this faculty works and what it is exactly. In the mean time, you know that you have at least 5 senses: taste, touch, smell, hearing, and sight. Some of us even claim to have a sixth: clairvoyance. The Seventh Sense that each of us possesses goes to that *sense of urgency and purpose* that gives us the ability to get things done in a much more expeditious manor than our peers.

So if you are ready, remember just one last thing; that creation, all creation, occurs three times in the universe; once in the mind of God, a second time when it manifests itself in your mind and then the last time is when it occurs in actuality. I have attempted to break this journey into bite size chapters for ease of digestion and to infuse in you an almost subliminal message. That message is that the greatest accomplishments are made by taking small single steps. When you have put lots of these little steps together, eventually you get to turn around and look back and see how far you have actually come. So let's begin this journey together. Deal?

1

Let's First Talk About Attitude

"So let's do it, shall we?"
"Do what?"
"Talk about attitude."
"I'm not sure I'm digging your attitude…"

There is a lot of speculation as to people having a good attitude versus a bad attitude and we even hear lots of people discussing how proud they are to have a "BAD" attitude almost as if to say Bad is in fact good. To them I say there is neither good nor bad (Yeah, you think I am going to finish the line and say "but thinking makes it so", but think again). There is neither good nor bad in an attitude because an attitude is whatever it is; the question is, will that attitude work for you? How effective will having your so called "bad attitude" be for you? Will it get you what you want or will it get you things you hadn't quite bargained for in the first place? There are other labels that one might hear being affixed to an attitude. One might hear of an optimistic attitude or a pessimistic attitude, a positive or a negative attitude, a "can do" or a "can't do attitude?" And all of this is simply to my way of looking at things, just another form of mental masturbation because none of these attitudes really speaks to one's effectiveness because of the limitations of **all** of these so called "attitudes."

Enter James Stockdale. For what is regrettably an increasingly diminishing number of Americans, there are very few who can answer the question as to who in fact this remarkable man was. He was I suppose, like so many of the other "giants in history", someone who disappointingly merely earns a footnote in American history. For me, however, he was not just a giant but a true hero, a patriot in every sense of the word.

I remember my first encounter with him: I flipped on the television in the early 1990's and I saw him in a debate; he was running for Vice President under Ross Perot. Now I am not ashamed to admit I was one of the few who made up the nearly 19% of the total voters in that election who actually cast their vote on the third party candidate with the big ears and the squeaky voice. Almost no one today will freely admit to this, to anyone, anymore, and perhaps this is because of the incredibly incompetent campaign that this winner of the Frank Purdue look-a-like contest ran. It was amazingly inept. The sad thing is that the issues and positions he took, for a good many of us, made a tremendous amount of sense at the time. Before I offer too ridiculous a political treatise let me come clean and tell you, that's really not the point. Let me just say for the record (and certainly everyone knows it): He lost the election! Third party presidential candidates in the United States always lose no matter how big a share of the ballot they get. The Republicans will tell you that a vote for Perot back then was really just a vote for Clinton and that is how Billy Boy got elected in the first place. But as interesting as all of this is for some of us, it skirts the issue of James Stockdale.

LET'S FIRST TALK ABOUT ATTITUDE....

So who was he and how did he find himself on the ticket? (Oddly enough, he would ask the same question of the American public and, almost in an instant, he would destroy any hopes of winning the nomination.) Like many of us who saw James Stockdale in his first interview on national television, if you saw it, you probably couldn't believe your eyes. This man who I described before as a giant, a patriot, and a hero, came across as, if I am to be polite, a tired old man who reinforced what we were thinking when he asked the question "Who am I and why am I here?" He was hoping to use this as a thought provoking opening line, but instead he came across as being a totally befuddled old buffoon, as if even he didn't know the answer to his own question. If I am to continue to be rude, disrespectful and unjust, he came across as a crusty old geezer who could hardly hear and clearly he could have given two cents about "playing to the camera." What is truly lamentable is that there had been no attempt to *package him* in any way. There were no "handlers" lurking in the wings to make the man who was to balance the ticket for the third party, appear to be anything more than what he was. This tragic attempt at letting the candidate speak the truth was both commendable in its innocence and ridiculous in its naïveté.

One has to ask the question; "What were they thinking?" Did they just plain **not** want to get elected? Didn't they know how things worked by now? This wasn't, after all, 1792, it was 1992 and there was a wealth of precedence that had already been established as to the power of this modern medium called Television. It made Kennedy, and destroyed Nixon. It celebrated Reagan, and parodied Carter, and it allowed Bill Clinton to charm his way out of an impeachment and get away with outright lying to congress and the American people. It is an incredible machine if one knows how to maximize its subtlety and influence. Oddly enough, the *boob tube* as it is sometimes called really can do an incredible job in proving what boobs we actually are.

Here was a person that was as "bottom lined" as ever existed. Perot picked James Stockdale to run with him in his race to the White House because he judged this man to be of the highest integrity and he thought that this should be more than merely sufficient to get him or anyone else for that matter elected. In a perfect world it should have been. But the world of the 90's was as flawed as today's. Our present reality is colored by so called "reality" TV shows that are so out of reality and Paris Hilton has become an American Idol which is as false as any of those clay idols littering too many museums' around the world. This too, is not to be confused with the show that has run for over ten years, "American Idol." These all too flawed impressions make up the images that continue to assault and shape our attitudes and influence the way we think and the way we act. But let's get back to Stockdale.

Part of his tragedy is that what he ultimately would become known for would be his failures (not his victories). To this point, he was so much more than a losing vice presidential candidate in 1992 under Ross Perot. Here's a list of just some of his accomplishments:

- He was an admiral and as such he was the highest ranking officer to be held prisoner in the Vietnam War
- In the years after his military service, he served (during the late 1970s), as President of the Naval War College.
- He was one of the most highly decorated Navel officers in American history receiving 26 combat decorations

- He also was awarded 4 Silver Stars and was a medal of honor winner
- He was a hero to his men and if not for him many more would have died during the 7 ½ years that he was in captivity

Fast forward: By the time he so imprudently accepted his position on the undercard of the Perot ticket, he was in fact a tired and broken man, broken by the years of serious abuses he had withstood in his cell in South East Asia; abuses he willingly withstood because it was the right thing for him to do and in so doing he would invariably become an inspiration not just to his men but to all of us. He spent four out of the seven and a half years as a Prisoner of War in solitary confinement and two of those were in leg irons and in the dark. And as grim as all of this might have been, these abuses and the others too gruesome to mention do not make him a hero. Let's be really clear on this point. No amount of suffering in and of itself makes you a hero. They might make one a victim, but it takes something else to move you into the hero category. What makes him a hero is how he conducted himself and what he did while he stood up to his captives.

Please stick with me because I am going somewhere with all of this. Let me give you a little more of the story and the pivotal point in this mans life; and that point, as he himself would later describe, was his time as a prisoner of war.

Its funny how life takes a detour sometimes, and for James Bond Stockdale that detour occurred while he was flying on a mission over North Vietnam. Let's give you a point on the time line. The date was September 9, 1965. He was forced to eject from his A-4E Skyhawk, which had been disabled from anti-aircraft fire. Parachuting downward, he landed in a small village, where he was severely beaten and immediately shackled. At this point both of his legs were broken. He was held as a prisoner of war in Hoa Lo for the next seven years. As I alluded to before, he was locked in leg irons (and placed in a bath stall). His nearly daily routine alternated between beatings and torture. At one point, (and here is where the heroism really begins to show itself), he was told by his captors that he was to be paraded in public not just for the purposes of ridicule and derision but for political purposes. He chose to slit his scalp instead with a razor to purposely disfigure himself so that his captors could not use him as a propaganda tool, as this was a common practice employed by the North Vietnamese at that time. This did not deter his captives so they decided to simply cover his head with a hat. Stockdale elected to kick this gambit up a notch and he beat himself senselessly with a stool until his face was swollen beyond recognition. He told them in no uncertain terms that they would never use him. When Stockdale heard that other prisoners were dying under torture, he slit his wrists and told them that he preferred death to submission.

(Collins, Good to Great) 1

"Ok," you say,

"So why am I telling you all this?"

Some of you may have read the best selling business book by James C. Collins called **Good to Great**. For those of you who haven't, it's a must read for anyone interested in business. I also think it will serve anyone well who wants to work toward having a successful life in general. In this treatise, Collins writes about a conversation he had with Stockdale regarding his coping strategy during his period in the Vietnamese POW camp.

Stockdale told him. "I never lost faith in the end of the story, I never doubted not only that I would get out, but also that I would prevail in the end and turn the experience into the defining event of my life, which, in retrospect, I would not trade."

When Collins asked him who didn't make it out, Stockdale replied:

"Oh, that's easy, the optimists. Oh, they were the ones who said, 'We're going to be out by Christmas.' And Christmas would come, and Christmas would go. Then they'd say, 'We're going to be out by Easter.' And Easter would come, and Easter would go. And then Thanksgiving, and then it would be Christmas again. And they died of a broken heart."

There is an apocryphal second part to this conversation that tells us that Stockdale then added that the pessimists were the second ones to go and that only the ones that knew what they needed to do, and in fact did what they needed to do that day to survive, were the ones that made it out. He concluded the interview with Collins when he said,

"This is a very important lesson. You must never confuse faith that you will prevail in the end—which you can never afford to lose—with the discipline to confront the most brutal facts of your current reality, whatever they might be."

Witnessing this philosophy of duality, Collins went on to describe it as the **Stockdale Paradox.** This will shape the background for a new philosophical construct on attitude and the essence of what we will discover is an underlying principal in harnessing the power of the Seventh Sense. But for now and from here I will expand on why I was originally going to call this book: "What a can-do attitude can't do." From time to time you may hear me refer to this as a Stockdalian attitude. For those of you that see it as a somewhat Stoic attitude, your observations would be fairly accurate. Because although Stockdale preferred the life of a fighter pilot over academia, he actually credited Stoic philosophies with helping him cope during the harshest years of his internment.

So as I conclude this chapter, let me say that the first piece of our puzzle in defining what the Seventh Sense is, is knowing what you need to do each day. And frankly, the only attitude that will get you through every time is a *realistic* one.

Certainly, there is always a place for positive thinking and I might even say that it is essential because without it "the real" conditions you might have to get through can become quickly overwhelming. But being the perennial optimist might be great for Pollyanna; just remember, however, that if the situation is harsh enough, an attitude like this might just kill you. And this is an opinion I will be happy to share with the late, great, James Stockdale.

Mega-ton Moment #1

You can't rely on a good or bad attitude. The only attitude that will get you through every time is a **realistic** one.

2

Let's Look at the Iceberg

We need to establish a little more ground work before we analyze your ability to begin harnessing your Seventh Sense. Many of us remember from grade school that an iceberg, which is nothing more than a giant ice cube floating in the ocean, is only partially visible to us. In fact **ONLY 10% OF <u>ANY</u> ICEBERG IS VISIBLE. THE REMAINING 90% IS BELOW SEA LEVEL.** So what does that tell us? Well if we use it for a handy analogy for human behavior we see that only about 10% of what people get to see (or know) about us is what commonly describe as whatever behaviors we manifest in our *skills and knowledge.* Everything else that goes into making us who we are, makes up the parts that lurks well below the surface and those are all the things that can be described as our:

- **BELIEFS**
- **VALUES**
- **MOTIVES**
- **JUDGMENTS**
- **STANDARDS**
- **ETHICS**

For lack of a better term, would it be wrong to call the sum of all of these parts, our attitude? If it isn't, then let's consider at an interesting mathematical conundrum? What makes your life 100%? You might find what I am going to demonstrate somewhat unbelievable.

Let's begin by assigning to each letter of the alphabet a value equal to it sequence in the alphabetical order, like so:

A	B	C	D	E	F	G	H	I	J	K	L	M	N	O	P	Q	R	S	T	U	V	W	X	Y	Z
1	2	3	4	5	6	7	8	9	10	11	12	13	14	15	16	17	18	19	20	21	22	23	24	25	26

Next: Let's look at some of the things we talked about that were on the last page. Remember we said there were certain things that could be observed by others and essentially these were above the surface of the water like the iceberg. Let's look at our **SKILLS.**

S	K	I	L	L	S
19	11	9	12	12	19

Adding them up your total equals: 82%
Not bad, but it doesn't add up to 100.

Let's go back to our chart and move on to our **KNOWLEDGE.**

K	N	O	W	L	E	D	G	E
11	14	15	23	12	5	4	7	5

Total: 96%
We're getting closer to 100 but we are not there yet.

Ok, how about **hard work**? Surely we have heard that there is no substitute for hard work. Guess what? I am not going to disagree with you but plug the numbers into the chart and see what you get?

H	A	R	D		W	O	R	K
8	1	18	4		23	15	18	11

Total: 98%

"Oooh", just missed it. But based on how close we got we can see how it trumps the other cards we've previously dealt to you. Ok, are we ready? Are you braced for impact? The only thing that will give you a total of 100% is **ATTITUDE.**

A	T	T	I	T	U	D	E
1	20	20	9	20	21	4	5

Total: 100%

So what this shows us is that our behaviors, all that is seen by others, which we manifest using our skills and knowledge, are ultimately effected by this thing we call an attitude. Having said this let's look at another kind of attitude: the Can-Do attitude.

How many of our teachers, mentors and parents have offered us encouragement and told us, "come on you can do it, you can do anything you set your mind to; **you CAN DO everything."** Were they right? Were they wrong? Were they lying to us? Were they offering us false hope? Or like the popular answer on all of those multiple choice question tests we took, maybe the answer should be "none of the above." Perhaps it should be 'all of the above"? Maybe we should really, in our Stockdalian way, insert a caveat? But I am not going to be the one who gets accused of raining on your parade. I will not tell you, "you can't do it" especially when NIKE has spent millions of dollars and told you to "just do it." Why? Because, I too, would like to believe that you can do anything; but let me offer you five words that make the axiom more effective when you add them. <u>You **can do** everything</u>: **but not all at once.**

Everything and everyone has limitations. And here's the best part. Even this general condition of a thing that we've been calling an attitude can actually be extremely limiting. Forget about going too far outside of ourselves for this one, because we even have a specific description for this condition; we call it a "self-limiting attitude." But what is so much more to the point and where we will be totally remiss if we don't introduce it to you now is: the notion of time. Unless we are omnipotent we simply can't do everything all at once. We have to choose. "Ah, (as Shakespeare said) there's the rub."

So many times we fail to make the choice that makes the most sense or is consistent with our goals. Here's a one of the biggest obstacles to being effective. It is becoming an increasingly pernicious ability for individuals in our society to have the ability to focus on one task at a time. The ability to "multi-task" is heralded as a panacea of talent and frankly a little bit of this particular skill-set can go a long way. The problem is that too many of us attempt to do everything all at once. This greatly diminishes our abilities to get anything done at all and none of it can be done well. Perhaps this is one of the reasons that one of the most widely diagnosed syndromes today is ADHD and more specifically Adult ADHD. Why this is, is unimportant but I am sure we could speculate that its prevalence is because of over-diagnoses today and under-diagnoses years ago. And so what? Let's deal with what we have to deal with now. People everywhere, seem to almost be chasing themselves, trying to be everywhere, in an effort to become all things to all people. Often times we hear of the "super woman" syndrome or working mothers trying to be "super moms" in an effort to cover not just all the bases, but bases that don't even exist. It is really kind of crazy if you think about it. But it would be unpopular to say "Hey people, why not try slowing down?" There are always limitations, as I said earlier, unless you are GOD. Even the angels are limited. They can't pro-create. They are neither male nor female. And even though they are faster than a speeding bullet, they can only actually be in one place at a time. How many of us overbook ourselves to the point where we want to challenge even the angels on this last task?

So if we can do anything but not all at once, what's the most effective way to get things done? The answer should be somewhat inherent in the question but let's just say it; one step at a time. How do you eat an elephant, one bite at a time? How do you set out on the proverbial 1000 league journey: by taking the first step, of course. How do you get to Carnegie Hall, practice, practice, practice? We all know these things but for some reason either we choose to forget them or we just plain ignore them, thinking that perhaps they somehow don't apply to us. Guess what, they do? None of us beats the rap on these concepts. So, slow down. "Make haste slowly." How about this bit of advice; "Easy does it." Friends of Bill W. will especially appreciate that one. And another one they will like and I think it might also be my personal favorite; "Let go and let God."

So whatever you are trying to get accomplished, lay out a plan and set your priorities and do it in a way that's **SMART.** That is to say: set **S.M.A.R.T.** goals for yourself.

- **S**pecific
- **M**easurable,
- **A**ttainable
- **R**ealistic
- And on a **T**imetable.

Let's take an example of this principal and apply it to our first Stockdalian belief system; "You can do everything but not all at once." Let's say you want to lose weight. After all, America is described as an obese nation, now isn't it? Great: for most of us, that is probably a highly commendable goal. But stating it that way means nothing and is very likely to never happen. So let's ask: How much weight? Let's say 20 lbs. Ok, now we are moving forward. That's a very specific amount. But, unless we decide to cut our heads off, we can't lose it all at once. This specific amount is also measurable. So far, so good. Is it attainable? We can't answer that question until we consider the time line. If we say we want to lose it in a week or two or even three that would neither be doable (realistic) nor healthy. So a SMART goal now begins to look something like this when it comes to losing weight. I want to lose 20 pounds in 6 months and I am going to do that by restricting my diet, eliminating sugar, decreasing my fat intake by 35% and by going to the gym three times a week for at least half an hour to 45 minutes each time. This is very SMART, very specific, measurable, attainable, realistic and on a very strict timetable. And guess what, we are not going to try to do it all at once.

Mega-ton Moment #2
You can do everything: but not all at once. Set Specific, Measurable, Attainable, Realistic goals for yourself on a very strict Timetable..

3
A World of Limitations

This next part will bother a lot of you, as I continue to build the framework for what the Seventh Sense is and how it can work more optimally in you. This will be so much so, that it will be like ripping a Band-Aid off quickly, so as to cause the least amount of pain. So, let me say it quickly. You <u>CAN DO</u> everything, **but there will be limitations.** Our American society has taught us, virtually from the womb, that this is not the case. And who can deny that our nation offers a world of possibilities unlike any other, perhaps limited only by our ambitions and the law of the land? Certainly, none of us likes to be told we can't do anything we set our minds to do and how many of us have had "our folks" tell us that we can do anything including becoming president some day if that is what? But is there any reason to not mention that for many of those that live here; this is simply not only not true, but not even possible. Doesn't our constitution have some serious restrictions on exactly who can be president? There is an age minimum and you have to born here. Those are some serious limitations right there. Based on those limitations, 60% of the population is not eligible. We see truly remarkable achievements on a daily basis, athletic feats that inspire us, people without legs running marathons using prosthetic legs; the list goes on and on. I play golf. But I didn't pick up the game until I was 50 and my reasons for playing are not the same as Arnold Palmers were when he was actively playing. When I first started, I told a golf pro I was taking lessons with that I wanted work toward being able to play a *nice social game.* I didn't want to go out and miss the ball. I didn't want to embarrass myself and if I could break 100 that would be great.

"Was that too much to ask?"

"It wasn't," was his response.

He went on to expand on his answer by adding one other comment, however.

"As long as you realize that less than 1 person in 20 can actually do that."

"Wow!" I said. "How is that possible? I hear so many people saying they shoot this; I shoot in the 80's or the 90's and…"

He cut me off.

"You have to realize, that a big part of the game is regrettably this thing called: LYING."

I was stunned. Later I learned how polite he was being and that everyone that plays golf knows that it is a game where you shoot 6, yell "FORE", and write down 5. Why do I tell you this at this particular juncture? It is because I think there is a great parallel here. Many of us lie to ourselves or worse we lie to our friends and colleagues. Hitler and his henchman took this concept and moved it to the level of the surreal and created the Big Lie theory and we all know what happened there. Ultimately all lies and deceptions catch up to us and the results run anywhere from disappointing to disastrous.

My daughter Alice is finishing up her undergraduate degree at the time of this writing and all college kids get tired of school by the 4ᵗʰ year. I like most good fathers who want to offer sound advice to their children, have stayed on her case and continually encouraged her to finish and get her degree. Too many young people today talk about taking some time off and "backpacking their way through Europe." That's a great thing to do too, by the way. But how many of those kids never go back and finish or it takes them 20 years to do so? Why? What is the **ultimate limiter?** How about that little thing called life itself? Have you ever heard the expression, "I was going to do this, or that, but life got in the way?" There is a great movie with Jack Nicholson and Morgan Freeman called the "The Bucket List." If you haven't seen it, I would recommend that you do. It wasn't the most critically acclaimed film when it was first released but it makes a great point for our purposes. It's about two old guys who are sharing a hospital room who both happen to be dying of cancer. As their friendship builds, they create a Bucket list; a list of all the things they would like to do before they *"kick the bucket."* The Morgan Freeman character is sitting there watching the TV show, Jeopardy, and he is relentlessly and correctly answering every question that pops up on the screen. Like a machine gun, he doesn't miss one. He tells us disappointingly that he had wanted to be a history professor. Based on his obvious intelligence this should have been a snap for him. But what happened? Life got in the way. He was going to City College after he got out of the army. Then he got married. Then he had a kid, then another, and the next thing you know life's limitations caused a road block that now became just one of the many regrets that he finally had to confront now that the last curtin was about to be drawn. Now, so many of you will argue that if it was important enough to him he would have figured a way to do it. And I am not going to argue with you on this either. But for ordinary people doing the extraordinary is either not possible or very difficult which is why we have to be mindful of those practical limitations that all of us have, all of the time. If I played golf morning, noon, and night, for the next 20 years, is it really possible for me to turn pro and take on the Tiger Wood's of the world? Well, that would be a BIG NO. Why? Because I have time against me; I am too old. I would be 70 by then. Plus I am not able to get that much time off even if I wanted to do that. There are physical limitations. Some of you might offer a host of platitudes?

"What the mind can conceive, man can achieve."

"Whether you think that you can or you think that you can't you're right."

I say, "What would Stockdale say?"

If you are in prison, all of the thinking in the world probably isn't going to get you out unless you have an incredibly well thought out plan. Remember the Count of Monte Cristo? He was in solitary confinement for what probably seemed like an eternity and still he was able to dig his way through solid brick walls after many years to meet up with a cell mate (from the adjoining cell) that would change his life forever. But he didn't just will himself through the solid walls. It took years. It was a Herculean effort. Ultimately when he had hoped to escape with his friend on the other side that plan had to be altered since his old friend, after years of abuse and malnutrition, in his very limited way, "chose" to die instead. Thankfully, this provided our hero, the future Count, with the means to actually make his escape from the island prison where he had languished for nearly 17 years. (Read the book to learn exactly how the gets out of prison.) It's a great story but as some will observe; it is just that, a story and no matter what, it is fiction, after all.

A WORLD OF LIMITATIONS

Let's consider some other limiting factors. A guy is driving around the back woods of Montana and he sees a sign in front of a broken down shanty-style house: "Talking Dog for Sale." He rings the bell and the owner appears and tells him the dog is in the backyard. The guy goes into the backyard and sees a nice looking Labrador Retriever sitting there.

"You talk?" he asks.

"Yep," the Lab replies.

After the guy recovers from the shock of hearing a dog talk, he says,

"So what's your story?"

The Lab looks up and says,

"Well, I discovered that I could talk when I was pretty young. I wanted to help the government, so I told the CIA. In no time at all as you can well imagine, they had me jetting from country to country, sitting in rooms with spies and world leaders; because no one figured a dog would be eavesdropping.

"I was one of their most valuable spies for eight years running. But the jetting around really tired me out, and I knew I wasn't getting any younger so I decided to settle down. I signed up for a job at the airport to do some undercover security, wandering near suspicious characters and listening in. I uncovered some incredible dealings and was awarded a batch of medals.

"I got married, had a mess of puppies, and now I'm just retired."

The guy is amazed. He goes back in and asks the owner what he wants for the dog.

"Ten dollars," the guy says.

"Ten dollars?! This dog is amazing! Why on earth are you selling him so cheap?"

"Because he's a liar. He never did any of that crap."

Forgive me for taking the time to tell this bad joke but I did so to make two points.

1. Sometimes what seems to be just isn't
2. Sometimes people (and dogs) just out and out…lie

Misleading facts or unreliable information goes a long way in influencing or contaminating your results. Unless the playing field is level and you are dealing with some empirical facts or fairly reliable information you will be significantly limited by what you were hoping for in terms of outcomes.

And here comes the slippery and paradoxical part. You will be constantly surprised at how people and institutions will consistently push this envelope of possibilities simply by what is no better described as "a shear force of will." The seemingly impossible will be brought into the world of not just the possible but the accomplished. So having said this, let's move on to the next point in our reality shaping process.

Something of equal importance and what almost serves as a corollary of our position statement that "you can do anything and everything but there are limitations," is the next statement: You <u>CAN DO</u> everything, **if it's important enough for you to do it in the first place.** So let's consider those of you that run for either exercise or as a leisure activity. I am not saying you shouldn't do this but I want to speak to those extremists that run marathons. But before I really address my personal feelings on this activity and why I choose not to engage in this formidable form of exercise allow me to give you a very brief history lesson. The name of the athletic long-distance endurance race, the

A WORLD OF LIMITATIONS

"marathon", comes from the legend of Pheidippides, a Greek soldier, who was sent from the town of Marathon to Athens to announce that the Persians had been miraculously defeated in the Battle of Marathon. The two places were not that far away from each other by 21st century standards but the distance of over 26 miles was not easily traversed and the fastest way to make a trek like this back then was to simply run there. Now based on the fact that this was seriously big news and it was important to get the word out, somebody had to do it. I am fairly certain that our friend Pheidippides had no inkling that people all around the world would be commemorating his feat thousands of years later and would be doing it as organized races with literally tens of thousands of participants. Certainly, places like Boston and New York that now have world famous marathon races didn't even exist when Mr. P was out there putting his best foot forward. In fact, he wasn't even racing anybody. All he simply wanted to do was go and tell people what had happened. It was the fastest way to do this since the telephone and telegraph weren't going to happen for about another 2300 years or so. But what most people fail to realize is what happened to our fleet footed Greek runner who was so hell bent in getting the news out: HE DIED. Let me say that again: HE DIED. So how crazy is it that people all over the modern world want to imitate this early newsman? Do they want to die too? Do they think that Pheidippides was enjoying himself when he was running along the rocky terrain (over hill and over dale) that one finds just about everywhere in ancient and modern day Greece?

Let's go back to the present. Have you ever noticed that all those people that are running marathons or running any kind of long distances don't really seem to be enjoying themselves? Look at their faces. Are they smiling? Not bloody likely, and if they are smiling while they are running they look like they are psychotic. No, they look like they are not having a good time at all. Every part of their face looks like they are either in pain or just plain focused on not showing they are in pain. Then, the best part of all comes. Are you ready?

Somewhere around the 21st and 22nd mile of the race just about everyone who runs marathons, I am told, has the same thing happen to them. They "hit the wall." This is an actual expression that has become a part of our every day vocabulary too and it is from running marathons that the expression evolved. Runners will tell you that at this point in the race everyone experiences a kind of physical and mental collapse that makes it feel almost like they have crashed into a wall. Gee, that sounds like a pleasant experience, doesn't it? So can anyone tell me again, I mean I must have missed it the first time, why does anyone want to engage in this activity? We said before, you can do anything, if it is important enough for you to do it. So let me make a personal proclamation to illustrate something. It isn't important enough for me and I am not going to do it; run marathons, that is. There I have said it and on this point I am done. I am not going to run no stinking marathons. I just don't want to and you can't make me. But you know what there are a lot of things I am not willing to do and are not important for me to do and I am sure you could make a list as long as mine and maybe even longer. So when it comes to this "Can-do attitude thing" thing I have been talking about, let's consider what is important, to you: Because it isn't getting done, if it isn't important enough. And if somehow whatever it is happens to get done, and it wasn't all that important in the first place, it won't be done all that effectively. The desire to get things done is crucial for its success. Numerous people could point out the benefits of running marathons to me if they had a mind to do so: the feeling of accomplishment, the fact that I would be in phenomenally better physical condition if I started running on a regular basis, the beta endorphins that would pulse through my brain as I experienced the now famous "runners high." All of those things become somewhat persuasive to me but my response is still.

"Crap, crap and more crap. I DON"T WANT TO DO IT."

It just isn't important to me at all. So when you are working on your personal action plan for life or business, remember if it isn't really, really important (to you) it isn't getting done.

With respect to running marathons let me tell you about two remarkable people: Mick and Phil. Now let's consider the fact that running alone is hard enough, so try to imagine running a 42K marathon while pushing someone on a wheelchair. This is an incredible story. Mick is the parent of Phil who is extremely disabled and in a wheelchair. His son, Phil suffers from Cerebral Palsy. His father Mick is a very accomplished runner and he and Phil have run many, many, half marathons/marathons over the years. Here's how it works. Mick pushes Phil's wheelchair. They aren't out to set records and their personal best is, I think, pretty phenomenal at 4 hours 12 minutes. In truth it is a very long way off from what the top competitors can do but for my money these two are tops in my book (no pun intended, since I have chosen to put their story in my book). I would urge all of you to go to their website and read about their unbelievable feats (and perhaps even make a donation to their cause.) http://www.micknphil-marathonlads.com/

So just how did they get started doing this? As Mick tells the story, his wife gave him an ultimatum in early 2002, "either take

Phillip in his wheelchair running with you, or pack it all in as, as I cannot cope any longer". He never really set out to be the fodder for a heart warming story it merely started out as one families attempt to deal with the day to day hardships of living. Well, based on this Mick had some simple and perhaps some not so obvious questions that included: Would the wheelchair stand up to it? Would Phillip like it? And most importantly, could he do this whilst pushing him and how much harder would the task become, as Phil would grow and mature since this would create addional weight which would have to be pushed? As hopefully most of my readers will have gotten or will get, he learned the answers to the questions as he embarked on this continuing series of journeys by starting off slowly and then by breaking it down into a series of pieces and steps. It started with a 2 mile fun run, which they clocked in at 17m 45s. Then they moved up to a 10k run clocking in at 46m. Next they tackled a 10 miler with a time of 1hr 48m. And then the ultimate challenge: the full marathon where they achieved a time of 4hr 12m. Here's the best part of this story, they were both loving it and quite simply, having the time of their lives and the rest as they say, is history."

I love these two guys. The story sends chills up my spine every time I tell it. And although "I" do not choose to run and I don't want to get involved with marathons it was important enough for Mick to the point where not only did he choose to take this route for himself but his heroism allowed him to forge a tighter bond with his son and he continues to do so each and every day. It's remarkable.

Now let me tell you a story about a woman I used to work with and I as I expand on this point hopefully it will become a little clearer for all of us. Her name was Joan and she was a top notch real estate agent. Every year I would sit with my agents and review their goals with them. We would look at their personal goals and their business goals. We would consider what had happened in the previous year, what distractions we expected in the up coming year, what kinds of things in general might keep us from achieving whatever goal we were setting for ourselves. One year she indicated that she wanted to learn to play the piano as a personal goal. This was something she always wanted to do and now that the kids were out of the house she wanted to get to this. This is something that was important to her for her own personal well being and in between running her business and being a good wife, a responsible member of my sales team, and an active member of the community; she wanted to address this long overdue goal. I thought this was great and highly commendable and I told her so. I lavished praise on her for it and told her how important it was for each of us to do things just for ourselves. I expressed to her how wonderful it was for our psyches and inner selves. Then I asked her.

"Of course, you <u>do have a piano</u> now don't you?"

"No," she said.

"Well, were you planning on buying one, or renting one or borrowing one? I continued to interrogate her on this salient point and explored other possibilities including gaining access to someone else's piano, maybe someone in some church group?

"No, she didn't have access to one," she calmly told me.

"You <u>are</u> going to get one then, aren't you," I asked.

"Yeah, I guess so," she responded.

Ok, let me tell you what happened next. I probably revealed a little impatience because the whole thing seemed so ludicrous and like so many other pipe-dreams that people frequently shared with me. This wasn't a goal. It was another time wasting exercise and sadly we both knew that this was never going to happen. And we would continue to meet for another five years or so before I would move on to consulting with Fortune 500 companies and Joan remained a very good agent and we have stayed good friends over the years. Each year I would ask her though,

"How are we coming with the piano lessons", or

"Hey, what ever happened with that dream you had to play the piano?"

Or "Did you ever get a piano?"

Regrettably we all know the answer. It just wasn't important enough for her. If it had been, at the bare minimum, she would have rented a piano and started to take some lessons. Neither of us will ever know if that effort would have paned out to anything remarkable. It was a thought, a pleasant fantasy, but little more than that. And this is not designed to be any kind of indictment because we all have these self deluding flights of whimsy. It makes us human. Taking them to extremes makes us silly and laughable Walter Mitty types. I am equally guilty as well. Here's one of mine.

I want to have a sailboat and one day become a skilled sailor. It's a dream right now and this is not to say I won't have one some day. I have even thought about writing an autobiographical book called "Sailing off Nantucket." In this mythological book I tell of some of the wonderful times I have had living on Cape Cod and enjoying a peaceful sail off the coast, crossing the various local whaling lanes headed toward the island that is so rich in nautical history and now is nothing more than a mooring for those that belong on "Lifestyles of the Rich and Famous." I am not sure any of this will happen, but it might, if one day it becomes important enough for me and somehow I choose to make the time to do all of the above. But for now I have other things that are more pressing and of greater importance so I must and will attend to them first. My dreams of a sailboat are just that dreams (and in no way are they goals) and hopefully there will be time for sailing later.

Do you have a burning desire? I was at a BNI (Business Networking International) meeting recently. The speaker of the day had his bio read by a committee member and that person went on to say that the speaker's "burning desire" was to sky dive one day. I thought to myself, "how absurd." How hard is it to sky dive, if that is what you want to do, just do it? What would it cost? At most it would be about $200. and it would only take either a morning or an afternoon to do it and it is done. What kind of a burning desire is that? It is a thought and nothing else. So either do it or not do it or call it what it is, an idle thought. How many of us go through life with hundreds of these snippets of dreams cluttering our thought processes? As you take hold of your Seventh Sense you will see fewer and fewer of these things happening. If it is important enough for you to do it, you will do it and simply stop talking about it. Your thoughts will convert to actions and your dreams will become a reality because they will become your meaningful and achievable goals.

Mega-ton Moment #3
You <u>Can DO</u> everything, but there will be limitations. If the goal is not important enough for you to go after it in the first place, then it will never get accomplished.

4
The Seventh Sense

Finally, we have arrived. As I mentioned in our introduction, most of us are blessed with at least 5 senses. Some of us have keener eyesight than others. Some of us might have a more finely tuned sense of hearing. Still others have what is described as a sixth sense or a faculty for being able to know things before they are about to happen. Their sense of intuition is empirically more developed than others and they can be shown to pick out cards in ways that seriously transcend random order. The CIA has special secret projects that are designed to harness this power and perhaps even at some point to develop weaponry that uses this force. But is there a 7th sense? There is indeed, and I first noticed it seemed that it was most discernable in the best of sales persons who seem to possess it in abundance. Without it, it was virtually impossible for them to rise above the ranks of the mediocre. Others can possess this faculty as well and for those that do, they are always seen at the head of the pack. They run businesses, foundations, and organizations: they are the ones that quickly find themselves in charge. They command respect immediately. It is at its core, the sense of urgency. It is that ability to see what needs to get done and for them to plot that daily course of action to achieve the goal.

Great salespeople know there are limitless reasons for prospects to offer "stalls" and or remain unresponsive. Somehow they are able to impress on their clients that sense of urgency that gets them to act. They simply will not allow a prospect to drift in the breeze and not commit one way or another. All well trained sales people are coached in various objection-handling techniques. They are taught to recognize the difference between an objection and a "stall." And when they are confronted with one of the classic stalls like,

"I need to think about it."

Their response will always be something like,

"So specifically what is it that you wanted to think about? Was it the price? Was it the delivery date? Please help me to understand?" What was it that you weren't exactly sure?"

It is too easy for them to not probe an all too familiar comment like,

"I need...or I want to think about it."

The one thing that separates great sales people is the ability to get their customers to respond, NOW. There is rarely any "Mutual Demystification." One doesn't have to be a sales person to use or possess this sense and having this sense always seems to amplify one's effectiveness. Let's take our weight loss scenario. You want to lose weight. When do you want to do it? The effective Seventh Sense possessing Can-do person will say, "Right now." They will consciously or unconsciously design a program that gets attended to now, not tomorrow or the next week, but right now. Sales managers everywhere are constantly reminding their teams to "close often and early" and get a commitment, in an effort to get customers to buy their goods and services as opposed to their competitors products. And as I said, it doesn't simply stop with people in sales. History is peppered with a myriad of examples of people who possessed it in abundance. Alexander the Great wanted to conquer the world. His Seventh Sense gave him the power to convince his generals that they needed to follow him to the ends of the earth and his sense of urgency allowed him to complete the mission in little over 10 years.

Back in the early 60's, didn't Kennedy promise the American people that they would have a "man on the moon" by the end of the decade? If he hadn't issued the challenge and set it on a relatively tight time line, he never would have made it. Even with focusing all of this nation's resources, he barely managed to squeak it by in July of 1969 just five months before his own self imposed expiration date. Regrettably, he didn't live to see it. But it was his sense of urgency, prodded by our nation's fear of falling behind the Soviets in the space race that made it happen at all.

Let's take a look at Czarist Russia in the early 18th Century. Dissatisfied with himself and others, Peter the Great spent his life trying to improve his outdated country as quickly as possible. Almost single handedly he was able to take a feudal country and move it into the so called modern industrialized world. His mission to carve out a country and open "a window to the west" was accomplished and it was because of his personal sense of urgency.

We see the same thing occurring in late 19th Century Japan. In fact, movie buffs will tell you that Tom Cruise's "Last Samurai" essentially tells the same tale. In that film we see the Emperor being forced to surrender to the reality that if his country is going to survive in the already industrialized world, certain traditions and cultural norms would have to be eliminated. The ancient order of the Samurai would have to go and he would have little more than a generation to get this accomplished. In a final shameful moment at the films climax, there is a bloodbath equal to that of the Charge of the Light Brigade and the fateful page of history is turned.

Of course, with respect to this notion, there is more than just the sense of urgency that we have mentioned. If we really take it to the nth degree, we begin to get to understand there is a deeper value, a more intrinsic essence and more profound nature to this sense: it is includes a personal sense of destiny. With this in mind, we need to consider something else. It is not an accident that from the word destiny we derive the word destination. So thinking about it this way, we need to constantly be asking ourselves the following questions:

"Where are we going?"

"Why do we want to go there?"

"Why is it so important for us to get there?"

The answers to these questions on a regular basis will help us to crystallize what is important to us. It forces up to focus on those things that really need to get done. And yet, the word "destiny" itself, tends to be somewhat scary and illusive to most of us. Rarely will you hear it used in common ever day language. Ask yourself,

"When was the last time someone asked you what your destiny was?"

How likely are you to hear someone ask you in a job interview the following question?

"So tell me about your destiny?"

But here's the deal, people with highly developed Seventh Senses actually do have a sense of what their destiny is. Even if they cannot put it into actual words, they see themselves as somewhat set apart from everybody else. They seem to possess an inner sense of "self" that drives them to transcend the mere here and now and it is this inner sense that allows them to constantly be driving toward their goals in an almost relentless manner. They are goal driven and task oriented. They are people of action who do not get easily discouraged. They are constantly on the move to get things done so they can move on to the next item. One of the ways they are easily discerned is they frequently walk at a faster pace, almost like it is a foot race. Actually, for them, it almost is. The have a clear sense of purpose and when one walks with them you had better pick up the pace so you can keep up with them. They may have a faster speech pattern. You will notice that in conversations they need to move things along. Patience is rarely their strongest suit and the stronger the Seventh Sense, the weaker is their own sense of patience. Oddly enough, they will frequently recognize this in themselves and set this as another task on their long list of self improvements.

To this end, the Seventh Sense person holds themselves much more accountable than the rest of us and constantly looks to improve all matters that affect them. Some other famous examples of these kinds of people would include; Benjamin Franklin, Leonardo DaVinci, Winston Churchill, and Teddy Roosevelt. Modern day persons like Hillary Clinton and her husband Bill to a lesser extent should also come to mind. I mention them here not because I was a fan or a supporter of either of them but just to give a clear representation of the characteristic I am attempting to describe. Neither is in my own estimation, a superior being, but their ability to take charge and stay on point was almost scary. For 8 years Hillary tried to get a health care program implemented during her husband's tenure in office and failed. Undaunted and relentlessly she took up the gauntlet and ran for president herself making it a key part of her campaign. After losing the nomination, she continued on as the appointed secretary of state under President Obama and helped orchestrate the program under him in the continued hopes of making it a reality. Most would have called it quits long before then.

The Seventh Sense then is that capacity to focus on what needs to happen immediately to get a task done and to stay on point. It is the ability to know intuitively what can be done and what cannot while still being able to place all limitations in their proper perspective so as not to mitigate an individual's personal resolve. It transcends courage, inspires both one's peers and subordinates and allows a person to withstand unusual amounts of ridicule while the process of getting the job done is being implemented through to its eventual completion. Succinctly put it embraces guts and foresight. The person who with the Seventh Sense is purpose driven at all times. With it the seemingly ordinary person is able to achieve what are considered to be extraordinary things..

"Make the best use of what is in your power, and take the rest as it happens."

Epictetus

Mega-Ton Moment #4
The Seventh Sense is the ability to discern what needs to get done, and how to get it done efficiently, while maintaining a sense of urgency.

5
The "Schmetterling Factor

So many times we elect to achieve something or set our minds to a task that is either not popular or perhaps even misunderstood. At the bare minimum, our peers and colleagues show us less than a hundred percent support. When this occurs, we frequently find ourselves adjusting our efforts. Some of us might actually cave under an assault of ridicule and simply abandon all hopes and scrap our plans. This reaction is all too normal and perfectly predictable and it occurs because of something I call the "Schmetterling Factor." Let me explain.

Many years ago I heard the comedian Orson Bean "do" a bit on the Tonight Show. Johnny Carson was still the host, just to put this event on a time line for you and how long I have been thinking about this. Orson was really a very clever comic with an easy going delivery and he became a standard on so many of the afternoon talk shows of his day. Clearly he was one of the regulars and "Johnny" loved to have him on and listen to his relentless banter. He was kind of like an erudite Robyn Williams without adrenaline. And regardless of who was on the show that night, when he was on, he managed to always round out the panel discussions. He became Johnny's perennial favorite along with the likes of Jonathon Winters, Don Rickels and Bette Midler. For those of you who aren't prone to staying up late, you may remember him in one of his more endearing roles as the shop keeper on "Dr. Quinn, Medicine Woman." Much like me, he professed his love of language and the idiosyncrasies of some languages over others.

One night he went on to make his point along these lines and said,

"Take the word butterfly. In English it is a pretty nice sounding word."

He then stretched the word and over-enunciated it,

"BUTTERRRRRRR Fly." It is a lovely word; you can practically feel its beauty as you envision these delightful little creatures flitting about from flower to flower in your garden."

"BUUUUUUUUUUUUTTER FLY," he repeated.

Continuing he told us, "and in Spanish it is even lovelier, the word is *mariposa*. MAAAAAAAAAAAARIPOSAaaaaaaaah."

And how about in French; the word is equally euphonic. "Papillion." He said it again two or three times each time slowly and methodically savoring every letter and each syllable: "PAPILLION, PAPILLION." Truly it is a lovely sound. Then he segued to the German word which is, *Schmetterling.* He over exaggerated the word and pronounced it in a comic guttural German tone and made it sound like one of the silly commands Sergeant Shultz would have given in the popular sit-com Hogan's Heroes. It was hysterical. He made further fun and shouted "Watch out, here comes the Schmetterling; run for your lives. We are being attacked by the flying Schmetterling!" I laugh to myself every time I think of it.

It was a very funny bit. It must have been because in 1999

THE "SCHMETTERLING" FACTOR

Tim Allen ripped the same bit off and gave it his own spin. You can catch it on

Youtube.com

Clearly it had an impact on me because many years later I was recounting this tale and one of the people I was speaking to happen to be German and as I built up the details and over accentuated each of the respective words in the various languages, getting laughs along the way, I got to the part where I said,

"and then in German, we have…", and then I was interrupted.

"Yes, Schmetterling, it is a beautiful word." Irmie, the German lady who was listening, further reinforced her position and added,

"It is a lovely word in my language." She repeated it slowly and easily concluded to all her satisfaction and declared,

"Schmetterling, yes it is a beautiful word." And to her it was. And the way she said it in a soft German polished accent, I have to admit it, but it sounded pretty to me as well. It wasn't funny sounding anymore. And from this story I derive what I call the *"Schmetterling factor." When people don't understand what you are trying to do or if it sounds funny to them, you will be the subject of ridicule and overwhelming derision. This mockery may become so extreme that it might make one change or alter their plans, adjust their focus, modify their intent or forget about the whole thing.* How much abuse do we think Christopher Columbus must have endured? He had literally been laughed out of virtually all the courts of Europe before he an Italian was able to get the ear of the Queen of Spain. I have a sneaking suspicion that he was only successful there because she found him kind of cute too. I think the idea of sailing west to go east was a little goofy sounding to her as well. Surely there were scores of counselors in Madrid saying, "Isabella, wake up and smell the paella." But Columbus never faltered. He would not be intimidated by the Schmetterling factor. Laugh away.

How about Edison? What about the Wright brothers? They knew what they wanted to do and what they wanted to get accomplished. Their ideas totally assaulted conventional thought. They had to sound like crazy people. Yet, they would not or could not be swayed by the naysayers and the scoffers. But let's think about this for a minute? They were all human just like us. Don't you think there were times when all of these innovators and achievers had second thoughts and when the voices all around them seem to be ganging up on them? Don't you think they were tempted to say something like,

"Yeah, they're right, this is crazy, what the hell am I doing here?" It would have been really easy for all of them to simply throw in the towel and surrender to the conventional thought of society. I am sure even most of their friends and family members were on the opposing side and by and large thought they were all nuts. All new ideas and attempts to change anything will be met with opposition and almost always with mockery and derision. People just don't understand sometimes. It sounds funny to them. It is as odd a sound as the word "Schmetterling" is to non German speaking people. Only the strongest and most resolute can get past this major emotional hurdle as they try to stick to their own Can-do attitudes and tap into their Seventh Sense. It's incredibly difficult for most of us. The average person is frequently unable to complete the task of achieving the goal they have set for themselves in many instances because of their own personal distractions. Add in the Schmetterling Factor, and most cave for sure... I like to think of this in biblical terms. It is said that there are certain evil spirits that could not be cast out unless they were called by name. So there you have it. I have given this devil a name and perhaps when your path is threatened along these lines, as indeed it will, you will be ready to cast him out too. You will call him by his name and say,

"Out, you Schmetterling," and simply be able to carry on. Some of us who have highly developed Seventh Senses easily withstand the Schmetterling factor. But others take solace in building this sense within themselves. Enter: Daniel Ruettiger.

Some of you may not be familiar with this guy so perhaps I should tell you the name that he is more commonly known by: he was nicknamed "Rudy." He was the real life character brought to life in the film of the same name who dreamed of not just going to Notre Damn University but playing football for the team known as the Fighting Irish. I mention him now for two reasons. In this chapter we are talking about the Schmetterling Factor and in the last chapter we talked about the ability to do anything but recognizing that there will be limitations. The Seventh Sense allows one to know what one's limitations are. Remarkably though the greater the presence of this sense, the greater the ability in one's own personal commitment to push the envelope and move those limitations to the nearly surreal. As such let me begin by giving you a little background on this courageous little fellow. Rudi had a hard time in school because he was dyslexic (which was undiagnosed until he was actually attending school at the junior college called Holy Cross. He grew up in a lower-middle class household, the third of fourteen children. So the possibility of him getting into a fine college like Notre Damn was indeed a long shot and the film did a pretty good job portraying this. But as it also turns out, he was quite the little football player, and I do mean little but fortunately for him while he attended high school at Joliet Catholic Academy, he played for locally famous coach Gordie Gillespie, and he led the team in tackles in both his junior and senior years. And, as the heart warming movie showed us, he was the classic example of the axiom "it is not the size of the dog in the fight it is the size of the fight of the dog."

But his dreams of playing for the big boys were laughable and the worst part is even those closest to him made fun of him. He suffered through not one, not two but three rejections to transfer to the University of Notre Dame, but finally he was accepted as a student in the fall of 1974. The fact that he even got in was a monumental tribute to his tenacity. His dream of playing college football was even funnier. I did say before didn't I; this was a little guy. But is spite of his being merely 5'6" and 165 pounds, he lucked out because at the time, Head coach Ara Parseghian encouraged walk-on players from the student body. I am not sure when Rudy found out about this about this but as an aside, if you consider the results of other long shots from this policy; Notre Dame's 1969 starting center, Mike Oriard, who was also a walk-on eventually won a Rhodes scholarship and an NFL contract with the Kansas City Chiefs. Having said this, I once heard that if you acted boldly "choirs of angels would come to your side." This very policy would give our little Rudi the angels he would need.

It's a great story and a better movie. If you haven't caught it, you need to put it on your must see list for your entire family. It makes me cry every time I see it. Getting back to the story, it turns out; Ruettiger gets to earn a place on the Notre Dame "practice-squad." They are kind of part of the team in that they help the varsity team (the actual team) practice for their games. In Ruettiger's last opportunity to move up to the real team and play for Notre Dame at home, Ned Devine who replaced Parseghian as head coach puts him into a game as defensive end against Georgia Tech (on November 8, 1975). He recorded a sack, which is all his Notre Dame stat line has ever shown. As the film ends we see Ruettiger being carried off the field by his teammates following the game. A footnote is added at the end telling us that Rudy Ruettiger is one of two players in Notre Dame's history ever to be carried off the field by his teammates. The other is Marc Edwards. Rudi Ruettiger: Laughable, limited, and undaunted by the Schmetterling Factor.

I remember thinking when I was watching the movie "what makes someone continue on, in the face of such a lack of support?" It was truly overwhelming. We watch this poor guy, suck it up for nearly two hours. This guy just can't seem to catch a break. And then there is one: he gets in to Notre Damn after three tries. Then he tries out for the football team looking like Mr. Peanut with shoulder pads and a bobble head and he doesn't make the team **but** he makes the practice squad. He accepts this present limitation (inwardly and perhaps subconsciously understanding that this brings him one step closer to his goal) but he still presses on and continues to dream of the impossible which is that eventually he will get the chance and suit up in the real uniform and actually get to sit on the sidelines. At this point it is as though he isn't hoping to play football for Notre Dame anymore because in his mind he already is. He just wants to suit up. Eventually he gets to do this too when they finally give him a chance to go in for one play, and then one more. 24 seconds of actual playing time and the dream is realized. Rudi overcame every obstacle in his way but in spite of the fact that on the surface his goals seemed ridiculous to everyone who knew him, in the true "can-do" Stockdalian fashion he did what he could do each day every day to get him closer to his goal. I would like to think that there is a little Rudy in each of us. There is, if we find him and we are courageous enough to look Mr. Schmetterling in the eye and tell him to take a flying leap.

Now let me tell you about Laura. Laura came to me when she was in her early 20's and I was running a large Real Estate office in beautiful downtown Orchard Park NY. By the way, that's the town commonly known as the home of the Buffalo Bills, for you NFL sports fans. I asked her, the same way I would ask all of my other agents from time to time a question that was designed to give me a reading on where their respective heads were at as it pertained to their personal book of business. Here's the question I asked her.

"So what do you really want to do when you grow up?"

Her response was so immediate and with such conviction that I have to admit she really caught me off guard.

"I know exactly what I am going to do. I am going to do this for two to three years and when I have enough money I am going to start my own Pet Spa business for Shelties."

Based on my own inner wiring I asked a few more questions to learn more about this dream, she so willingly shared with me. I did not indicate in any way that I thought it was foolish or far-fetched. I always think it is unconscionable to do anything like that. So let's fast forward again shall we.

A little more than 10 years later, little Laura LaCongo has just opened her second state of the art facility. She is not only one of my star business coaching clients but she has two stores;

one in Dallas and the other in, you guessed it, beautiful downtown Orchard Park NY. Her *La De Da* line of doggy grooming
products includes, lotions, potions, shampoos and colognes and
includes such snappy labels like "Who's your Daddy." One thing
for sure, this girl is truly someone to watch as her franchise literally goes global. I easily see her becoming the next Mary Kaye
(for the dog world). I am sure they chuckeld at **her** too as she
was stirring and mixing up her cosmetic line at the kitchen table.
She gets to have the last laugh as well on this one, since the Mary
Kaye product is number 3 in customer loyalty behind Google,
and Avis. But perhaps I should finish this important section by
telling you one last story.

There once was a bunch of tiny frogs, who arranged a running competition. The goal was to reach the top of a very high
tower. A big crowd had gathered around the tower to see the race
and cheer on the contestants... The race began... Honestly, no one
in the crowd really believed that the tiny frogs would reach the
top of the tower. You heard statements such as:

"Oh, WAY too difficult!!"

"They will NEVER make it to the top." or:

"Not a chance that they will succeed. The tower is too
high!"

The tiny frogs began collapsing. One by one...Except for
those who in a fresh tempo were climbing higher and higher...
The crowd continued to yell

"It is too difficult!!! No one will make it!"

More tiny frogs got tired and gave up... ...But ONE continued higher and higher and higher... This one wouldn't give up! At
the end everyone else had given up climbing the tower. Except
for the one tiny frog that after a big effort was the only one who

reached the top! THEN all of the other tiny frogs naturally wanted to know how this one frog managed to do it?

A contestant asked the tiny frog how the one who succeeded had found the strength to reach the goal. It turned out... That the winner was DEAF!!!!

The wisdom of the story is this: Never listen to other people's tendencies to be negative or pessimistic... because they take your most wonderful dreams and wishes away from you. The ones you have in your heart! Always think of the power words have. Because everything you hear and read will affect your actions! Therefore: ALWAYS keep faith that you will prevail in the end. Rudy did, and so did Stockdale. You can too. And above all: Be DEAF when people tell **YOU** that **YOU** cannot fulfill **YOUR** dreams! If you are beginning to feel your Seventh Sense growing within you, it is very possible that your sense of hearing is diminishing at the same time. It must be so.

"I'm sorry. What was that you were saying?"

Mega-ton Moment #5

Keep the Schmetterling factor in mind! Be DEAF when people tell you that you cannot fulfill your dreams and keep faith that you will prevail in the end.

6
Being the Best?

I suppose upon reading this opening question some of you want to break out and beat your chests and revel in your own sense of greatness and that's a good thing. But here's where I attempt to knock you down a peg and shift into my Stockdalian mode once again because now I am going to tell you something else which will seem to be limiting. You know that your Seventh Sense is working when you accept that **you CAN DO** everything, *but you may not be the best at everything*. So many times we see people scuttle themselves in search of the Holy Grail of perfection. As a part of the Can-do philosophy that I hope you will come to embrace, and as you begin to harness the power of your own Seventh Sense my assertion is that being the best can become a dangerous scenario indeed. One reason for this is the shear allusiveness of this quest. I call it the "fastest gun in the west syndrome." As nice as it might be to say that you are the fastest and as much fun as it be to be the fastest, it can also do two things that are totally destructive. In the end it can get you very, very dead and the other issue is the fact that there is always someone who is going to be a little faster. If this isn't true today it will certainly be true tomorrow. Getting yourself in the record books is a grand thing but since all records are eventually broken some people actually can be frozen and fail to act, thinking to themselves, "What's the use?" To my way of thinking this lends itself to the worst kind of self limiting belief system. Worst still, the tragedy of it is, is that it is all too common. This philosophical construct is based on the premise that when it comes to getting things done one should strive for greatness rather than being the best. Perhaps I should modify this last statement and say rather than "settling" for being the best. To be great is always the goal for me.

To make this point, let's look at sports figures for a moment. Let's consider Mohammed Ali. It can be argued that as good as he was he was not the best heavyweight boxer we ever had. He was not undefeated. Rocky Marciano, by contrast, had a record that was significantly better and he is the only champion to retire undefeated. So does that make Marciano the best? Oddly enough some of you true sport fans will recall just prior to the Rock's death they made a computer enhanced video where they pitted these two giants against one another to see if the brawler could beat the dancer. It was made using a combination of actual footage from both fighters' careers, input about their individual strengths and weaknesses, and they actually had the two men do some individual fighting in the ring. (Marciano was well past his prime when they shot it so they actually had to have him fitted with a toupee to make him look a little younger for the camera.) It was as fascinating as it was revealing because at the time Ali was still fighting and was undefeated.

BEING THE BEST?

We will never know how it would have turned out if both of these titans were in their prime and actually met in the ring but the results the computer generated for us showed that indeed the Brockton blockbuster would have come out victorious. Based on this conclusion it became handy fodder for the last of the Rocky movies (Rocky Balboa) and they imitated the results using today's technology. In the film it forces the actual title holder (Mason "the line" Dixon) to ask Rocky Balboa to come out of retirement to determine who really was the best (so that everyone could know and the argument could finally be put to rest.)

The Marciano and the Balbo stories make for interesting parallels and serve my point well because as interesting as all of this might be for any of us, the more valuable issue becomes garbled and convoluted. It really isn't about being the best at all, because that argument will never be settled. Here's is what cannot be disputed. All of these men were "great." Greatness can never be taken away from you. If you are great, you're great, it's that simple. For my money Mohammed Ali truly was the greatest. This man was poetry in motion when he was in his prime and for me he represented one of the finest specimens of human athleticism I have ever seen and probably will ever see. And the best, past his prime, in his greatness, doesn't diminish Rocky's (Marciano that is) greatness at all. They are both great. That's the best part of being great. It is its own category and once you are in the annals of greatness you have arrived and no one can take it away from you. Let's take O. J. Simpson for a moment. He was one of the NFL's greatest running backs of all time. No matter what infamy follows him afterward his greatness remains. Some will argue that he is a despicable guy who literally got away with murder and I might even be one of them; but on the football field he still remains one of the great ones.

Mohammed Ali is worth mentioning again as we talk about what I describe as the illusion of being the best. When he first started out he launched a major public relations campaign and got himself well established on the map of pugilism. He barked at the media and told them he was this, and was that, he was the prettiest, he was the best and eventually he concluded for everyone that he was simply the "Greatest." Frankly he thoroughly pissed off an awful lot of people along the way and very few initially bought any of the malarkey he was throwing at them. Oddly enough at this point in his career if anyone was the ambassador for the power of positive thinking it was Ali (Cassius Clay at the time) because he "grew into his own greatness." The funniest part of the story is that in the beginning even he didn't believe his own ranting. It was just a way for him to continue to build the gates. His constant harangue of "I am the greatest, I am the greatest" became a self fulfilling prophesy for him. After a while, even <u>he</u> began to believe it; and you know what, he became that much better and with every fight his improvement was clear to everyone. With Ali the story gets even better. A terrible thing happened to this warrior athlete. At the height of his career when his physical ability was absolutely at its zenith he elected to not let the American government draft him into military service and he was stripped of his title and barred from boxing. We know now that eventually he would be vindicated but the man who bench marked greatness and literally saved boxing from an ignominious ending as a sport was sidelined. We will never know just how great he could have been if his career had not been interrupted and this is for a guy that later on would come to define legendary greatness.

But hold on a minute. This is where his saga and his legend really just begin. Up until this time what made him great was his speed, his ability to "float like a butterfly and sting like a bee." He was incredible. A three year layoff would rob him of this. As great as he was, when he came back, he lacked speed and grace and if it wasn't for that thing that lent itself to his ultimate greatness he would have become another sad story in sports; the story of the aging fighter who stays in the game too long. It was the second stage of his career that most of us remember. After his legs were gone, he introduced what he called "the rope a dope." With this new and deadly strategy he would go on to vanquish his toughest opponents. And vanquish them he did. Let's take the infamous and very scary George Foreman. Thirty years ago he was one very scary dude. It is difficult to imagine him then when we see him today as that big jolly guy hawking his George Foreman Grills. When he was first champion and in his 20's he had virtually run out of guys to beat up. Few went more than 2 rounds. He had terrifying punching power and when he stepped into the ring with Ali who was attempting to make a very tough comeback, few gave Ali a chance. Most expected Ali to get a serious whipping from the much younger and stronger Foreman. This was the guy who could literally stop a freight train with his punch. He reminded me of Clubber Lang (played by Mr. T) the fearful opponent in Rocky III who the Burgess Meredith character described as being unbeatable and one who could "knock you to tomorrow." Here's the best part Ali recognized this and he knew full well that his own legendary speed was gone and his legs would not let him float like a butterfly anymore and he told everyone in the press exactly what he was going to do to beat the young champion. He was going to give him the "rope a dope." Since the champ (Forman) had almost never fought anyone for any duration and rarely over 10 rounds, Ali was simply going to "lie on the ropes" and let the "younger and stronger" Foreman literally punch himself out. When he was really tired Ali was going to retaliate. Guess what? That is what he did to the letter. He "roped the dope" in and let him beat himself, and when he was exhausted Ali moved in for the kill and knocked him out. It was beautiful and no one could believe it. So what's the point of this story?

It goes to what we have been saying about tapping the power of the Seventh Sense and knowing intuitively what one needs to do and what changes in strategy need to occur. You have to know what you can do and what you can't do. If Ali couldn't dance he was forced to figure away to maximize his own solid heavyweight punching power. He did not try to use powers he no longer had. All of the positive thinking in the world wasn't going to give him his speed back. The butterfly was finished. He would have to gather his own resources as a slugger if he was going to survive now that his ability to move was gone. Now certainly he wasn't planning on going toe to toe with anyone but he would be able to cover up for a number of rounds and come out and swing against an exhausted opponent. The rope a dope was brilliant. I loved him for this because he shows us all what we need to do: we need to use the tools we have when we have them. When they are gone we need to look for new tools that will work and accomplish what we need to get done. They might not be the same tools. They might be totally different. We may literally have to recreate ourselves in the process but we need to do whatever it takes even if we have to redefine what makes us who we are. Mohammed Ali is for me the champion's champion.

> "First say to yourself what you would be; and then do what you have to do."

Epictetus

Mega-ton Moment #6

When it comes to getting things done, striving for greatness will get you closer to your goal then simply striving to be the best. You <u>Can Do</u> everything, but you won't always be the best at it.

7
You Can Do Anything

You can do anything, but you will need help. If your Seventh Sense is working, you know this already. You are neither afraid to admit it or ashamed of the fact. We have all heard the expression, "No man is an island." So many of us fall prey to the *lone wolf* school of getting things done and when we are left standing there in the cold, alone, not getting things done the way we thought we would, we get to boast about "how we didn't need anybody to give us a hand," or "I didn't need anybody." Well, I suppose to some that might be an extremely commendable attitude and I guess I might add a resounding, "kudus to you" for your sense of independence. Unfortunately, more times than not, I would be compelled to add a giant "so what", as well. In my coaching practice I never cease to remind my clients; it's all about results. I will ask them repeatedly.

- "What do you want to achieve?"
- "What do you need to do to achieve it?"
- "Whose help will you seek?" And most importantly;
- "Did you achieve it?"

How one gets there is so much less important than if the mission was accomplished. Frankly, one of the keys to *ineffectiveness* is trying to do too much without the proper support. The D-day invasion would not have been possible without the ships, and the LST's (the landing craft that were commonly referred to as Large Slow moving Targets). Without air support, the inordinately high casualties would have been 5 to 10 times worse. Can you imagine trying to play basketball with only 3 men on you team as opposed to the correct number of 5? Kids growing up, when they first learn how to play basketball quickly learn the term "ball hog" and resist the impulse to ever be called one because it shows that you are not only self centered as a player but that you don't care about your team winning as long as you can be the showboat. Everyone hates a ball hog. It almost guarantees a quick loss for any team.

Is there anyone out there that thinks Luciano Pavarotti or Placido Domingo just woke up one day and could sing the way the do? They had countless teachers, a myriad of vocal coaches, and a host of mentors. Even track stars that run their races all by themselves invariably have veritable armies of strength and conditioning coaches, and teams of trainers. We have all heard "there is no *I* in team," haven't we? Why; because it is true. No one gets anything done of any consequence if they have to go it alone. Let's think of Michelangelo and the famous Sistine chapel. Granted the lion's share of the work is credited to him. But he had all kinds of help. Do you think he built all the scaffolding all by himself? Who helped him organize his paints, take care of the routine clean up, and attend to his personal needs? Sure, they make up what is probably scores of unsung heroes but I will bet you at the end of the day the painter said "Thank you," to somebody. Let's not forget the guy who hired him. If it were not for the vanity of Pope Julius II, there would have been no Sistine Chapel and it wasn't because the pontiff ever even dreamed of raising a paint brush himself. If you take away only one thing from this treatise it is this: the biggest obstacle to success is not seeking out the proper support when you need it at each step of the process. One also needs to acknowledge that they are only a single link in a long and uneven chain. As you begin to develop and use your Seventh Sense you will be unafraid of not only asking for help but you will become relentless in its pursuit. In the most extreme cases it will even seem like one is simply using others for their own gain. Be warned on this point. In the more nefarious kinds of people this is inherently true. Hitler, Ivan the terrible, Idi Amine, and Stalin are just a few examples of those who not only seemed to harness the darker sides of this force but who amassed sizable armies of followers committed to their evil causes.

Mega-ton Moment #7
One of the keys to *ineffectiveness* is trying to do too much without the proper support. You <u>Can Do</u> everything, but you will need support.

8
If You Don't Like Something

If you don't like something, change it. If you can't change it, change your attitude. Don't complain. The most significant change in a person's life is a change of attitude. A "right," or an effective attitude, produces a right action which leads to results. Putting it succinctly then: Attitude, leads to actions, leads to results. When I first started to synthesize this sytem and understand the inner workings of the Seventh Sense I actually considered referring to it as some kind of an Action approach because nothing occurs in the universe, to paraphrase Einstein again, without action (movement). But if all action is influenced by attitude it would make sense then if a change in attitude could create or influence a change in action, then of course, magically, the reverse will also be true. The problem that arises, and I must add regrettably so, is that rarely do people ever find it possible to do what I call "change gears." Enter the lasagna story.

See if you see yourself in this story. Marjorie, a friend of mine from many years ago, told me she had an aunt who used to make her crazy. She would complain about how she had to make the lasagna for Sunday dinner and what a pain it was. She would have to roll out the pasta and get it ready and get the ricotta cheese from the store and brown the chopped meat…but then she would have to make a separate batch because Nickie and Joey and the kids were coming over this week and they were super fussy, and she wasn't sure how much to make, I mean she probably could freeze some if they didn't eat it all and everyone knows leftover lasagna is really the best anyway, and, well you are starting to get the drift on this saga by now. My friend's Marjorie's aunt would pretty much tell her a version of this same story every time she saw her and she would patiently listen to her because her aunt was older and it was respectful. One day Marjorie, who clearly was in the process of emerging as a modern woman and getting her *consciousness raised*, got it into her head that she was going to try something different. She was going to challenge the status quo for all time and as you have surmised: It was time. She couldn't take it any longer. She asked her aunt when she began the usual diatribe,

"Aunt Lou, what would happen if you just didn't make the lasagna? I mean, it seems like an awful lot of work and it obviously makes you very upset and clearly it is an unusual amount of work and we are not sure if anyone really appreciates what you have to put yourself through to get the lasagna served to all of them. I mean, am I right or wrong?"

The response was immediate and probably to most of my readers predictable but it truly caught poor deluded Marjorie off guard because she would tell the story for years to come and give us all a great laugh. In fact the retelling of the story actually gives the story meaning and without it we have the simple babbling of an older woman. Aunt Lou looked at her in total disbelief, horror and bewilderment and probably was disappointed at her niece's sense of disconnection and she said,

IF YOU DON'T LIKE SOMETHING

"What's wrong with you? Haven't you been listening to a word I have been saying? I **have to** make the lasagna, Joey and Nickie are coming over and they were bringing the kids and everything, and people are just expecting her to make the lasagna, I mean what would happen if they didn't have lasagna, what would they eat, I can't believe you don't want me to make the lasagna, what could you be thinking? Not make the lasagna; how ridiculous?"

That's the lasagna story.

It might have a painful ring of familiarity for some of you and although it clearly shows part of my Italian upbringing you can probably substitute any kind of food or any other kind of scenario that shows how sometimes some of us get ourselves in such an attitudinal rut that we cannot conceive of ever getting out of it. It would shake us to our cores. The reality is so strong it is without question. It goes beyond a sense of tradition into almost a twilight zone kind of reality. The worst part is it all makes sense to us. It is the way it is. And yet, I say question away. If it isn't working for you, if it isn't getting you to the goal you are trying to achieve you must make a change in either attitude or action. Which come first is a highly debatable point and frankly it makes no difference as long as you make that detour. Personally I think a change in action happens first and when we see that no one has died we take a second smaller action and then we begin to develop a newer attitude of possibility and before you know it, we enter the world of Seventh Sense Can-do. For some of us it is a world of salvation if we can in fact make the change; if we can take the leap. Unfortunately, there are so many more of us who are just stuck and it is a tragedy. Life is short Bunkie. If we are all destined to get only a quick "three score and ten" we had better figure a way to tell and live a few less lasagna stories if we are to get what need out our lives. And one last thing to remember too, no one wants to listen to the lasagna story either. But I will bet you knew that didn't you? Well anyway, I certainly hope you knew?

Mega-ton Moment #8

If you don't like something, change it. If you can't change it, change your attitude. Remember: An effective attitude produces a "right" action which leads to results.

9

If You Really Want to Be Happy

If you really want to be happy, nobody can stop you. One of my favorite quotes, and I don't know when I first heard it, was "Tragedy and unhappiness are inevitable, misery is optional." I am beginning to gain a sense that some of you are going to think that this is going to be the lead-in for an excerpt from "Chicken Soup for the Soul." It isn't intended to be that at all, but I suspect it might sound like one. So if it does, please forgive me or at least try to put it in the context for what it is we are trying to get accomplished here: to give you a new position statement that will begin making you more effective and help you get what you want out of life by getting you to tap your own Seventh Sense. We have all heard stories of how people have risen above extreme adversity and inspired others to do the same. When I was a child I was constantly being reminded of the person "who cried because they had no shoes and then they met a man that had no feet." It is a poignant story and it reminds us of what's really important. It serves to give us what I consider to be one of life's greatest gifts: the gift of perspective. So many of us go through life and become side tracked or preoccupied with things that seem to be important until one of life's "events" shows us where we should be placing the highest value.

I get so tired of listening to the moaners and groaners, and all of the relentless complainers. I suspect you do too. I often think if they really had problems they would have legitimate reasons to complain. Have you ever asked yourself, "why is it that the people with a reason to complain rarely do?" Many years ago, I worked with a Real Estate agent who kind of became a cartoon character because of her constant "woe is me," nonsense. People who were forced to listen would frequently get caught rolling their eyes whenever she would begin. Let me call her Pat.

Pat was actually a very accomplished Realtor and had a great book of business and she made a lot of money. She drove a great car, lived in an incredible house; she had a husband who was a saint and what really frosted most of her peers is that she got the lion's share of her business from Relocation referrals. For those of you who aren't in that business, what that in effect means is she did not have to prospect for the lead. It was handed to her. Now granted she would have to pay a hefty referral fee for the client but for most people in Real Estate that still makes for an incredibly sweet deal. The clients were almost always very high end (the cream of the crop) and in what are known as being in "must buy" situations. They were rarely "maybes." Pat would go on and on and tell anyone who was willing to listen how hard she worked (as if she was the only one that did.) This was especially annoying because the other agents had to scurry to get their own leads and earning significantly less than Pat. She would continue with this effrontery and complain to them, how on occasion she would have to take her customers to lunch and they simply expected her to pay. This would also go over like the proverbial lead balloon since everyone was faced with the same kind of expectations.

The *coup de grace* would always come and she would inevitably lose her audiences when she would begin to regale them with what I call the **devastation** stories. As the sales manager I was treated to at least one devastation story a week and I would follow it up with "my" response. The devastation story, or perhaps I should say, the devastation series, went something like this.

"I can't believe it. You have no idea how hard I worked with these people. I must have shown them 50 houses (the actual count was always closer to around 8). I drove them through the Northtowns and all over the Southtowns, I took them all over downtown and played tour guide. I bought them lunch and dropped them off at the hotel. The worst part was they had an awful little brat of a kid who wanted ice cream so who do you think had to get the little creep a cone? You guessed it, me. I never saw the parents reach into their pockets once. Of course, she (the little brat) got ice cream all over my car. I just don't get people sometimes. Then after two days they tell me they have decided to not take the job after all, and that the parent company in Cleveland is going to move them to their offices in San Diego instead. Can you believe it?"

(NOW HERE COMES THE BUILD UP. Are you ready?)

"I was devastated."

Then the tale of woe would move from just kind of sad to truly annoying. Pat would work herself into a complete lather, and feed her own "devastation" to the point where she would work herself practically into tears.

"It is just awful" she would say.

And she would go on and on and proceed to wail and rant and rave and tell me how upset she was. I suppose in my total maleness I neglected to be as compassionate about Pat's need to vent as some of you might be thinking. She wasn't looking for an answer or a solution; she just wanted to share her frustration. Perhaps I misunderstood this or had lost any sense of caring because these sorts of conversations would happen WEEKLY. And WEEKLY she was devastated. It was beyond aggravating especially when one considers what can and should be described as devastating. Famine in Africa is devastating. The world wide Aids epidemic is devastating. The agent that I had down the hall from Pat whose husband was in hospice with cancer, might be allowed to use that word but I really found Pat's raving difficult to listen to each and every week and frankly I thought it was an incredible misuse of emotion. It was just wrong.

On occasion, I would get sucked in and in a fatherly way try to reassure her and get her to see that she needed to put the situation in perspective and understand that I could sense her frustration…but in truth, nobody DIED, did they? She simply had a customer "not buy." Unfortunately, these responsorial strategies would help for only for about 15 seconds or so. There would be a sniff and a snivel, but it never really did much good and she would come back with, "but you don't understand." The only dividend that came out of it was that when things became mildly frustrating for me around my own house, my wife and I would tell each other how "devastated" we were and smile and move on to resolving whatever needed addressing. But Pat <u>never</u> got it, and as a result she never could really grow as a person and would remain the self absorbed bore that everyone knew she was. So let me say it again, "…unhappiness is inevitable, misery is optional." She opted to be miserable. It was her choice. My choice, if I was to keep her selling was to suck it up and have to deal with her habitual lamentations. In every other respect, she was a good sales person, so I made the deal and quietly sighed about once a week for about 9 years. Enter Beverly Sills.

For opera buffs the mere mention of her name brings a smile to their faces. They think first of her remarkable talent and how she made New York City's Metropolitan Opera House the place to be when she was in town giving one of her incredible performances. They smile a second time I suspect, because, I don't know or can hardly think of a time when I can recall Ms. Sills not smiling. Her smile would electrify audiences. She was one of the most charming and pleasant people I ever saw. Her laugh was like a series of bubbles bursting and many would think that is where she got her nickname.

Yes, Beverly Sills was called "bubbles" by her closest and dearest friends.

And now as Paul Harvey would say, let's go to the rest of the story. Beverly Sills' talent on the stage was matched with a life that was beyond tragic in her personal one. Her first child was born with severe birth defects and Beverly the trooper that she was never complained and just dealt with it and continued to be an incredible wife and mother, while at the same time taking her place as the queen of the Opera stage. Well as fortune would have it the good Lord smiled on her and gave her a second chance at having a sound healthy child. Not that she loved her first child any less but don't we all say, "We don't care if it is a boy or a girl, as long as they're healthy." Only those that have suffered the challenges and pains of a special needs child know what Beverly would have to endure on a regular basis. Oddly enough many of them would also share with us the fact that we can never know the joys they share as well. So as life would have it, she delivers a second child and this time the news is worse. The extent of the challenges are so much harsher and the difficulties are almost without measure. Deafness and blindness are only the starters. I ask myself how one deals with tragedies of this magnitude? What a trooper. She was her usual cheerful self and she loved her baby and carried on, in what became her signature legendary style. On the way home from the hospital she has the baby in her arms (this was in the days when seat belts and baby seats weren't required) and is trying to comfort her when her car turns up the driveway and starts heading toward the house and she looks ahead and can see the flames billowing from the windows of her house. She looked down at her baby, more than likely gave a thought about her other child and the tough road that lie ahead there. Then she looked again at the fire consuming her home, gave a furtive glance to her husband and they both began to laugh.

There is a Yiddish word; a mensch. It doesn't need much translating but it means something like a person who you really want to know. Beverly Sills was a mensch. She was never down even when the world would throw everything at her. She was unflappable. She couldn't seem to help herself. She was who she was and as such she was as light as soap bubble, and that is the story of how she got her nick name, *bubbles*. I don't know where some people get these inner reserves of strength. I am sure that in that moment she probably laughed a bit and cried at the same time as if to say to God,

"Is there anything else? What more can you throw at me, Lord?"

What she didn't say was "Oh my, I am devastated."

That's why the name of this chapter asks the question, "If you really want to be happy…can anybody stop you?" Some people have trouble understanding the thing we will call: the state of happiness. Sadness is in the healthy human, a transient emotion that all of us should feel in response to things that make us sad. If we are sad all the time we have the condition known as clinical depression. I wasn't in the car with Beverly Sills but I know she had to have had her heart filled with sadness to the point of breaking. But her natural state was to be happy and nothing and no event could take her from that place. I think it is easier for some of us and indeed it is a blessing but I am convinced that my God, the loving God that I have come to know wants us to be happy. Sure we will be visited by things that will rightfully tip the emotional scales and force them to sway one way or another. That's the deal. But let me tell you about another very special person: My Aunt Mae.

My mother was an identical twin and many times we affectionately referred to my mother as being the evil twin. She wasn't evil at all. In fact, she was a very good woman but she was certainly full of the devil sometimes and she was also a fish monger's wife. She cursed like one too. Her identical twin sister, Mae was the opposite. She was quiet and soft spoken and literally never had a bad word to say about anyone and she was one of the people that forces us to ask the age old question "Why does God allow bad things to happen to good people?" She had a terrible life. Granted she had glimmers of happier times but to my way of thinking she had things happen to her that went way beyond the pale. She could not have children of her own, so she and her husband Mike went to a little orphanage in Montreal and they adopted a lovely little girl who would become my cousin Lorraine. She was beyond adorable. Let's fast forward. In Lorraine's teen years she became involved with drugs and ultimately 20 years later she would die a miserable death hopelessly addicted to alcohol and methadone. Making matters worse, Lorraine would have a child who would follow his mothers course and would die similarly (of a drug overdose) when he was just 28. Now for the record my Aunt Mae was one of the finest mothers I have ever known and together with my Uncle Mike you could not have met a nicer more loving couple. The Chinese have a curse: "May you outlive your children." Wow, that is pretty awful. If you are a parent, it truly, truly can't get any worse than that. The irony and the extra sting of giving a childless couple a child only to have them watch the tragic demise of that child, and then the subsequent death of the grand child, is something that is totally unfathomable to me.

My Aunt Mae mourned the lose of these beloved people. She suffered the anguish of their individual battles with their addictions. But she never wore their sufferings as a badge of honor or held herself up to say "woe is me." Never. If you didn't know what was going on in her life, you didn't know. She was an inspiration of suffering. I always felt blessed to be in her presence. If you want to be happy no one can stop you. She proved that to me, time and time again. On her death bed at 85 years of age she had some final laughs watching Seinfeld in her hospital room. I always laughed at Seinfeld when the show was running and I still tune in and catch the reruns now and then. The members of that ensemble have taken a special place in my heart for bringing some merriment into the heart of someone I loved and cared for so very deeply. Some of us, I think, are put on this earth to help others see a better way to live. Some of us are put here to cheer those up who are going through tougher times. There should be a special place of esteem in our society for those that go around and cheer people along and offer them a respite from their grief. My Aunt Mae inspires me to this day and Jerry Seinfeld makes me laugh. They are both important.

Enter Sullivan's travels: There is a great John Sturgess film which was made in the 30's called *Sullivan's Travels*. It's about a famous movie director who makes screwball comedies for a living and he has become famous for doing so. He's frustrated. As an *artiste* he feels he is not using his talents appropriately and he needs to go and make the Great American Movie. He needs to make a film that has substance, which will move people, a film that will establish him as one of the great film makers of all time. To do this, he decides he must get close to the people that come to see his films. So he elects, in a very *Prince and the Pauper* way, to go out in disguise and walk among the people. Now let's think about this for a moment. This is the height of the Great Depression. As the film unfolds we have a host of comedic scenes of the studio people following him about trying to not be seen by him, carefully taking up watch over him so he doesn't get into trouble. They continue to frustrate him in his individual quest for him to find his personal inspiration. He finally gets his way and he convinces the studio big shots that they have to leave him alone and stop following him. He must be left to his own devices so he can "walk among the people" and really find out what they are like and what the secret of life is. Perhaps this is where the hidden message of the film is "be careful what you ask for, because you just might get it."

He gets his wish in spades. The studios cut him loose and he walks among the people only to find himself in the wrong place at the wrong time, without any money and any identification as to who he really is, he gets arrested and he is subsequently sent to prison after one of the speedier trials that most poor people in this country have come to expect. Now prison was probably a lot less fun in those days than it is now (it's all relative). Corporal punishment was standard procedure with bullwhip floggings. The food was close to being inedible and the living conditions were beyond deplorable and the only thing one had to look forward to was getting up the next day to endure further hardships. At the brink of his despair, when there seemed to be no escape, there is a glimmer of a respite from his misery: it's movie night. The irony of the scene is the movie he is going to see with the rest of the prison population starts out with a cartoon and everyone watching nearly wets their pants laughing. They thoroughly enjoy it with uproarious laughter which I suppose was contrasted with what they were forced to endure each and every day and it made the cartoon seem that much funnier and that much more enjoyable. Our hero is in awe at the magic he sees in the faces of the convicts as they are transformed if only for a few moments from hardened criminals to child like people in a brief oasis in time. If only for 20 minutes or so; they are relieved from their perpetual misery.

Well as luck would have it, he finds a way out and gets back to the studios and resumes his former life. This time his great American movie is going to be a bigger and better screwball comedy (just like before) because he realizes how important it is to make people laugh. He realizes that too many of us lead quiet lives of desperation and that his mission in life was to help lift some of us up from the depths, not from depression, but from depressing circumstances. Life can be a bear sometimes. I have told you of two people in this chapter who life almost seemed to go after with a vengeance. They didn't bring it on themselves.

IF YOU REALLY WANT TO BE HAPPY

It is what happens. Beverly Sills and My Aunt Mae had terrible things happen to them and yet they were able to smile through it all and bring joy to the people around them. For some of us, I think we get a sacred charge to help people put one foot in front of another when times are tough. Our hero in Sullivan's travels got that. Jerry Seinfeld may not have thought of his work as being a sacred charge but he does know how to make people laugh and for me that's pretty important. It is the ultimate form of encouragement. Here is one of the things that is crucial for all of us who want to understand one of the more important aspects of their usage of their Seventh Senses. It is difficult or impossible to be made to feel "Up" all the time. Sometimes we need to laugh. Sometimes we need to surround ourselves with people that can make us laugh. We need to laugh at ourselves and our circumstances. If we don't, it may not kill us but it will make us less effective in accomplishing our goals. A second part of this is knowing what is important and what drives us in the end.

"Difficulties are things that show a person what they are."

Epictetus

Mega-ton Moment #9

On the road to your goal, you will be met with obstacles and bad things will happen. It's inevitable. That being said, it is your choice to either let these bad things make you miserable and deter you from your goal, or make you stronger and retain a positive outlook.

10

What's in Your Glass?

We've all heard a version of the axiom, "Whether a glass if half-full or half-empty depends on the attitude of the person looking at it." It seems that everyone wants to divide the world into glass half empty and glass half full people. Wouldn't it be great if we could just truly pigeonhole everyone and be done with it? It is rarely that easy. Following this sophomoric logic, I always like to say if you ask someone from NYC the same question they will probably respond with something close to,

"Hey, quit looking at my glass, stupid." or "Who the hell stole my glass," and "Don't even think about grabbing my glass, buddy."

Either way, dividing the world into a "this way or that way" scenario is supposed to address the difference in the way people look at the same facts. It's that, "Are you part of the solution or part of the problem", mentality. We can go round and round on this one and it serves little purpose. What is important is what you are going to do about it. Let me revisit one of my favorite Creative Problem Solving (CPS) techniques as we continue to expand on our silly half empty (or should I say half full) glass. The technique is called "What", "So What", and "Now What."

The absolute "What" is we know one thing for sure: we have a glass at **50% capacity**. There is no emotional label fixed to it. That is an empirical fact. We are most likely to have the opportunity to make progress when we stick to measurable facts and eliminate emotional tags. Following this line of logic we ask the second question: So What? Well depending on what we are hoping becomes our outcome; we can ask an almost infinite number of questions and create a so what indeed scenario? Here are some choices.

- I am not that thirsty, but I will finish drinking the rest of the water, I suppose?
- I wish I had more water I am really thirsty.
- I wonder if there is any more water.
- What happened to the water that was in the glass (presuming it started out as full)?
- Who spilled the water out of my glass?
- What should I do with the remaining water in the glass?
- Where can I get more water?
- When should I go to see if I can get more water?
- Is the water in the glass potable?
- Should I ration the water I have left?

You get the drift. I don't know what one expects from our simple glass but we could continue with this situation analysis ad infinitum. This leads to the most important part of our exercise: The "now what."

"Now what" will allow us to move from ineffective labels through situation analyses to serious strategies that give us a multitude of options that could create acceptable outcomes? The "Now what" options might include:

WHAT'S IN YOUR GLASS?

- Let's figure a way to get more water?
- Let's figure a way to get rid of this water?
- Let's use the water to water the plants?
- Let's use the water to brush our teeth, wash our face, shave, etc.?
- Let's figure out whose face we can throw the water in?

Using this method you will perhaps have noticed the introduction of yet another "invitational stem": let's figure a way. The "let's figure a way," approach redoubles our effectiveness because it not only addresses the myriads of possible options we might have at our own disposal it allows others to join in the process and they can and will make addional suggestions we never would have even begun to have consider. Use this method whenever you are forced to confront an either or problem and you will realize that the situation has a multitude of options. Ultimately it will help you become your own Yogi; Yogi Berra, that is.

It was Yogi who told us that "when we see the fork in the road, take it." Now you might chuckle at this simplistic logic but it really speaks to one of the most critical pieces in the effectiveness puzzle; being decisive. One of the most important characteristics of highly effective people, who are using their Seventh Senses at optimal level, is their ability to make decisions quickly. I like to call this: a "Curlyism." For those of you who don't remember the character in the film "City Slickers", Curly was the leathery cowboy played by the late Jack Palance. In a pivotal moment in the film he tells Billy Crystal and his sidekicks that in life if will always come down to: "one" thing. He states this in a decidedly defiant manner by holding up his index finger and gesturing to each of them. Their fearful response is,

"Well, what is it? What's the one thing?"

"That's for you to find out." He tells them menacingly.

If you do nothing else: be decisive. Too much depends on this and the decision to not make a decision is a decision. One thing for sure: the decision to not make a decision is usually the worst and most costly choice one can make. I call it the Hamlet decision.

Many people have heard of Hamlet and the play that bares his name. Some even know the famous line "to be or not to be" but might have forgotten who said it and to what it refers. Fewer people really understand what the play is about. Here is my spin on Hamlet. Hamlet is a Danish prince who is given to moodiness but the one inalienable *tragic flaw* of Hamlet is that he is terminally indecisive. This poor guy couldn't make a decision to pour water on his head if his hair was on fire. For 5 acts we watch this poor schmoe, wandering around his castle saying things like, "should I go see who this ghost is or should I not see the ghost, should I kill my uncle who is banging my mother or should I not, should I kill myself or should I not (that's the whole, "to be or not to be" thing; to be dead or not to be dead, and what would happen if I was dead? Would my situation be even worse)? This game of mental ping pong leaves a score of dead people all over the stage by the end of the play. In the end, even he dies; "hoisted on his own petard" as they say. So my suggestion is "make a bloody decision" because the decision to not make a decision will in fact be much bloodier for you virtually every time. Use whatever creative problem solving techniques you can find. Know what you want in the end. Be true to yourself and your Seventh Sense will guide you and keep you from living in the ineffective world of indecisiveness as it compels you to set and deal with each deadline after careful consideration of all of the acceptable and unacceptable possible outcomes.

Mega-ton Moment #10

The decision to not make a decision is usually the worst and most costly choice one can make. Decide to be decisive! If you are decisive and true to yourself it will allow your seventh sense to guide you and inform the choices you make with effectiveness and efficiency.

11

There Is a Better Way for Everything

There is a better way for everything; find it. I believe in my own Stockdalian way that I will prevail in the end and that there is always a better way to do something or a better way out or that there is something else I can do to improve my current situation. I also believe in social, spiritual, and physical evolution. There is so much that is both good and bad that has been written and said about this word, evolution, that Darwin capitalized on, but in the end I think that everything is striving toward a constant state of improving itself. The philosophically difficult question as to why God allows bad things to happen to good people is ultimately answered for me in that the bad thing that is occurring is designed as one simple link in the chain that is destined towards ultimate improvement. The key is we get to make choices and we get to look for ways to change and improve the things or events that are occurring. Nothing stays the same. One of my favorite quotes is that "Change is the ultimate process of all living things." I would like to tell you that this was something Gandhi said. It would be profound if I told you that Jesus said it or even Albert Einstein. But unfortunately it was that bastion of logic himself, Mr. Spock, from Star Trek fame. As such, we, for those of us who choose to begin to harness the power of the Seventh Sense; we have an obligation to always be looking to make things better by actively choosing the processes and strategies that go to improving the systems or the events that confront us. We discussed the half empty and half full glass scenario in the previous chapter. Let me share an equally banal statement. There are three kinds of people: those that make things happen, those that wait for things to happen and finally those that sit around and ask,

"Can someone here, tell me what the hell just happened over here?"

Obviously the group most of my readers will want to be in is the first one. This presumes they want to be using their Seventh Sense. Their Seventh Sense will force them to always be looking to improve their current situations. The status quo is anathema them. One of my favorite lines in Collins treatise "Good to Great" has to do with this very premise. He boldly declares that "The enemy of great is good." For most people, "good" is just that: it's good. For Collins and those who will clearly be able to manifest their Seventh Senses, "good" is anything but good. For them it merely becomes a license to remain at a level that most will deem to be satisfactory and, that which, they must transcend. "Good" for them is considered to be something that is either mediocre or simply average. It is an instance or an event that is little more than a simple single point on the time line that later will lead toward excellence or higher standards.

Mega-ton Moment #11

There are three kinds of people: those that make things happen, those that wait for things to happen and finally those that sit around and ask, "Can someone here, tell me what the hell just happened over here?" Make things happen and find the "better way".

12

The Big Difference

The big difference between a successful person and others is not a lack of knowledge, but rather a lack of will. History is not just revealed but made by people who have had the will to do things when others have not. These days we hear of green power, solar power, thermal power, wind power, nuclear power, but is there any greater power in the universe than ***will power***? God himself created us as a function of His will. Without His will there is nothing that exists, not even the Big Bang theory. Whether you believe the story of the fall of man or not as it is recounted in the tale of Adam and Eve, it all revolves around the issue of will. When we were cast out of the Garden of Eden, as the story goes, we did so as a consequence of our free will. It might be argued that we chose badly but this is of little account, so let me make the point by discussing a somewhat apocryphal retelling of those events. There is a version that mentions that when man was created he was given two choices; happiness and free will. He chose free will so that he was able to choose his own happiness. We have reviewed this in previous chapters and by now I think you may have been convinced that if you want to be happy nobody can stop you. Now mind you; you cannot simply will it to be so, but you can, by the virtue of your free will, choose it to be so.

One of the things I learned growing up as a Roman Catholic was how we can exercise this faculty of free will. Catholics have a familiar signature tradition of fasting and abstaining from various foods at various times (like Advent, Lent and on certain Fridays) and these observances serve two purposes: they serve to give us the opportunity to offer reverence to God and they also provide us with the ability to *exercise* our will. To give up eating meat on certain days is not all that difficult (especially for someone like me who would eat fish everyday if he lived in Florida) but at the minimum it takes an exercise of will. How many of us are there who have tried to go on diets or give up smoking only to find that we lacked the will and invariably we have as they say in Alcohols Anonymous, "a slip?" We might find ourselves going for that small piece of candy or taking just one drag from someone else's cigarette and we feel doubly guilty not just for having succumbed to the temptation, but more significantly because we showed ourselves to be so weak willed. People who are strong willed are always respected, sometimes admired and often they are even feared. Why? Simply stated it is because the world is made up of weaklings and lily-livered wimps. My contention is that it is because most have poorly developed Seventh Senses. Ironically we find many of these "less than effective" types frequently rising to positions of control and leadership. Again we ask, how can this be and the answer lies in that thing called the Peter Principal (where all men rise to the limit of their incompetence). How could those that are weak not be threatened by the strong?

I find it to be additionally ironic when we hear children being described as willful (or bold) and strong willed. It is as though the parents have abdicated the responsibility of their own authority. The statement almost is made to serve as an admonishment or to warn other adults to be careful that their *"**despot in training**"* is a person to be reckoned with when they, the parents, in fact are not. After all, who is the parent? Adding to these series of paradoxes, we also have gender biases when we get to the subject of will. A woman who is seen as willful or strong willed is frequently viewed as nothing more than a "bitch" while a man is considered to be forceful, dynamic, and authoritative (as opposed to being authoritarian.) The so-called glass ceiling in business is only beginning to get shattered in many circles and the authoritative (strong willed) woman is finally getting a chance to take her rightful place in Western Society. (Although I was not a supporter of Hillary Clinton, I would like to say here and now that I found her to be 1000 times smarter, more resolute, and capable than her husband on his best day. Her Seventh Sense was truly a force to be reckoned with and it continues to be so. Regrettably, however, I think her forcefulness worked against her many times solely on the basis that she was a woman. It is disgraceful for us as a nation that this should be the case and doubly embarrassing that in the 21st century in this country, people still ask the question,

"Should a woman be **allowed** to be president?"

The ancient Aztecs are noted for their incredible astronomical ability, the accuracy of their calendars, and of course their abhorrent practice of human sacrifice. On the lighter side of this culturally diverse group was the way they viewed people who drank too much or who were involved in other practices that would be described as a profligate or a free wheeling life style. They were seriously condemned and often times ostracized and prohibited from taking part in the usual Saturday night blood letting rituals. The attitude of these Mezzo-Americans was diametrically opposed to the one we see in the 21st century. People who drank too much were never considered to be alcoholics. They were never treated as if they had a disease. No quite to the contrary, they were thought of as being weak willed and as such they were social pariahs. Their culture reinforced the black and white nature of things. There was good and evil, dark and light, and weak (willed) and strong (willed). My personal feelings on this lead me to think that in many ways our Aztec brethren were closer to having a more optimized society than we can ever hope to have with our current thinking. Today no one appears to be responsible for anything anymore. We have socially unacceptable behaviors by the score and we have become very comfortable labeling them as diseases and this is designed to have the offender totally abdicate all responsibility for those behaviors. If you are sexually profligate, you get to go to a 12 step program for sexual addiction. If you are hot headed, you can go to a rage anonymous support group. If your appetite is out of control, why not go to over-eaters anonymous. No, no one is responsible anymore. The weak (not the meek) are clearly being assigned to the role of the "inheritors the earth."

Some of us are old enough to remember the great comedian Flip Wilson. He simply said jokingly that the "Devil made me do it." I won't comment on the existence or the strength of Beelzebub's persuasive talents but when did we stop having the ability to use our will to make a better choice? It makes me kind of angry and I would like to think it makes some of you angry too.

Let me give you another case where this concept of will undergoes what I can only describe as relentless perversion. Some of you might remember the story of the lady who put the cup of coffee between her legs after going through the drive through at McDonald's. The salient point is she got burned or scalded more specifically because the coffee was too hot and she wound up suing the giant hamburger chain for several million dollars (ultimately settling for in excess of two million). What the hell ever happened to personal accountability or responsibility? She willfully put the coffee between her legs and yet it is McDonalds fault. How pathetic is that? Are you ready? And now we have the rest of the story. 20 years later, more or less, her daughter does the same thing and she sues McDonalds again and collects about a half a million. How nuts is that? Now I know companies are frequently held hostage by would-be litigants and many lawyers will advise us that it is so much cheaper to settle these kinds of nuisance cases "out of court." Some will even tell us that "business is business." My response to this is we live in a society that fosters these kinds of aberrant behaviors. Our culture has stripped us from all accountability. Should we be upset at judges who allow these kinds of rulings? That might not be a bad start but the problem has so permeated our American way of living that there more than likely is no turning back. Don't believe it? Than consider this. There is a website called www.WhoCanIsue. com. There are billboards all over Florida directing you to the site and by the time this book is printed they will probably dot the entire Eastern Seaboard. Isn't that just grand? Surely we can all find somebody to sue around here, now can't we? All we have to do is check our consciousness and our consciences at the door. While we are at it, we should relinquish all personal responsibility and deny the existence of our free will. Is that such a small price to pay when we can "sock it to the man" and make a fast buck?

You have to decide that one. Unfortunately most of our society is going for the cash.

In the mid 80's I bought a wonderful farmhouse high on a hill in a town called East Aurora, NY. It had 30 acres more or less and steams and woods and ponds and for a kid from NYC it was a little bit of heaven. There was a lovely little family that lived there and they were selling it because the man of the house had died and his widow, Marge, was not able to keep the place up any longer. I come along and bought the place and 30 days before closing her son Mark was tragically killed in a car accident and I and my, soon to be, bride just figured that we would never close and poor Margie would just have to be institutionalized because of her incredible grief. Let's think about this for a moment. The poor women, loses her husband and than less than 6 months later her son dies. Grief like this is too much to bare for many and we presumed the worst and psychologically we were all set to move on as we extended our condolences. Well as it turns out the seller, Mrs. Yacobuci had emotional reserves that many of us do not and we closed on the property exactly when we were supposed to and she simply moved on with her life. Now it turns out that when we looked at the house that spring we noted a number of really nifty things about the house. There was a delicate corner hutch built into the dining room. There was a fabulous field stone fireplace. There was even oak parquet flooring in the living room. The parquet could be seen bordering a tasteful oriental carpet and appeared to be in great shape. When we ultimately closed it seemed that she had graciously left the oriental behind and we said to ourselves, "Gee, that was very nice of her." When I lifted the carpet to do some vacuuming I discovered that the parquet flooring that I had admired did not extend under the carpet at all. The carpet merely was covering the sub flooring. I smiled and said to myself, "oh well, it's not the end of the world," and moved on. I cannot begin to tell you how many people suggested to me, in extremely emphatic tones by the way, that I should sue the seller. In my heart of hearts I cannot think that this poor woman was trying to pull a fast one on me. Even if she was I had an obligation to discover things for myself, didn't I? If I had known what was under the carpet it would not have changed my position at all: not one bit. Now certainly it could be reasonably argued that this could have been construed as a **known latent defect** and as such both she and her agent had an obligation to disclose this?

But each time I chose to discuss this with my so called friends I could not wait to go off into one of my tirades and counter with,

"Listen, I am a smart fellow, I have a Real Estate Broker's License, and if I was that concerned about it, I suppose I would have looked at it before I bought and it would have been my choice to say or do something, right?" I go on to tell them,

"You know there are special places in hell for people who go around and add to other peoples misfortunes just because they can."

I chose to exercise my free will and not take the offensive even though I had the right to do so. I was then and continue to be accountable to myself.

When I teach contract interpretation to Real Estate practitioners, I always underscore the three most important things they will find in any contract; the legality, the reality and that all important thing called leverage. I suppose I might have had some legal justification to make a stink to the poor widow. The reality was that I could have discovered it for myself if I had a mind to do so. Certainly as my friends might have argued she might have made an attempt to conceal it (I think there was no malicious attempt here at all and I choose to hold her blameless and let me underscore once again in case you didn't hear me the first time; <u>I didn't care</u>). The issue of leverage can be readily introduced and I chose not to be an idiot over this even if there were various courses I might have taken which might have included;

- filing a complaint with the Real Estate Board against the listing agent
- filing an action in Small Claims Court against the seller

But having the ability to do things or the leverage to do so doesn't give one the obligation to be an idiot. I made a conscious choice to exercise my will and I chose to ignore it and live in the house happily ever after. I mentioned the website <u>www.whocanisue.com</u> before. Is there any reason that lawyers have become the butt end of jokes for so long? My favorite one is

"What do you call 10,000 lawyers at the bottom of the ocean? Answer: A good start."

Is it an accident that Shakespeare tells us in his play "Julius Caesar" that,

"We need to kill all the lawyers?" Our society has paid a very high toll because we have embraced this "skin people when you can" attitude and the "that's what the law is for," mentality. But it all starts with the will to do so. So go ahead and ask yourself:

- What will you do?
- What do you want to do?

THE BIG DIFFERENCE

- Are you justified in your actions?
- What difference will it make and to whom?

Afterwards you might want to ask yourself one more question. Was it worth it?

Mega-ton Moment #12

You have free-will for a reason. Use it and decide what you want, and how you will get it, if your choices matter and to whom they will make a difference, and if your choices are worth it in the end.

13

Where You Are Matters

You <u>Can Do</u> everything, ***but where you are matters.*** If your Seventh Sense is well tuned you are aware of this fact and you humbly acknowledge it. I remember when I bought my house in East Aurora NY back in 1985. A number of people questioned my about my sanity. They said things like,

"So let me get this straight, you moved from NYC where you had a thriving business, and you came to (Buffalo) a depressed area, you came here without a job and you bought a house, just like that; are you stupid or crazy?"

They would frequently mollify their position statement, seeing that I was deeply offended by the question no matter what form it appeared and it was not because of the former or the later inference. So they would add,

. "Or do you just have an incredible pair of balls?"

My response was usually something like,

"Well let's think about this for a second, I came here as a college graduate, I had and continue to have a strong work ethic, did I mention that I also happened to have a Real Estate Broker's License. I had a few bucks in my pocket, I am a healthy white adult male and am blessed to be living in the United States of

America the greatest country in the world; it takes little in the way of courage to make that work, if I can't make it work with all of those things working for me, shouldn't I just be ashamed of myself?"

I would go on to instruct my assailants about the history of our country; how men with much greater courage than I came to our shores with nothing. They were many times in ill health, uneducated, with no money, many times being unable to speak the language and yet they went on to forge out a wilderness and build a great nation. That, I would explain, took courage. How much easier is it to make a success in a business in the United States today than it would be (given the same set of circumstances) to do so in Bangla Desh? How much easier is it to get an education here than it is in Haiti? How much easier is it to have a happier life in America than it would be to do the same thing in China, New Guinea or Albania? Where you are makes a difference? This is not to say that opening a business in Shanghai is impossible, it is just easier in the U.S. One will find that regardless of how you look at things there are fewer (or more) challenges in one place as opposed to another. The same thing can also be said of the times that we live. Now in this particular instance there is virtually nothing you can do about it and the entire Seventh Sense and can-do thinking thing won't change anything.

But let's consider something. I can remember seeing the musical Les Miserables. It is a great evening in the theatre based on the Victor Hugo classic which tells us of the incredibly bad times the French had to endure during the French Revolution. It is a tale that has been told and retold and there have been numerous film versions; some good, some not so good. Perhaps it was the music that presented me with a different reality with this subsequent retelling of the story of Jean Valjean. As I was watching I could not help thinking about just how bad their conditions were and what these poor French people had to live through during these tough transitional times. Let me underscore this for those of you who did not see the musical, read the book or who are just not students of history. <u>They were living in incredibly bad living conditions.</u> Ironically, they weren't just having a bad day, they weren't just having a bad week; these people were having a bad century. Now while they were going through it there is no way they could have extricated themselves from their own reality and said,

"Not to worry, things will be better a hundred years from now."

But I could not help thinking that how unlike the Irish, the Italians and even the Germans were compared to the <u>French</u>. Here's the difference. When conditions got really awful for everyone else they elected on their own to do something about it. When the potato famine hit Ireland and the population of the Emerald Isle was reduced from 11 million to about 3 million, nearly 17,000 died making the crossing to America. My Irish ancestors said something like,

"Get me the hell out of here."

When conditions got bad all throughout Europe in the late 1800's virtually every nationality said lets go to America (or Canada, or Australia or somewhere else where life can be better.) Granted now not everyone made this decision but literally millions did and the immigration stats on Ellis Island will pay testimony to that fact. But not the French. They just hunkered down and took it. Now I suppose their tenacity is commendable and even extremely praise worthy. I just think,

"Heck man, get me the hell out of here too."

When the Welsh coal mines became exhausted most of Tom Jones's (the singer) ancestors said,

"Which way to America?"

One of my favorite quotes is that you should

"Bloom where you are planted."

One of the great things about being a citizen of the world is that with courage and a little fortitude you can also uproot yourself and re-plant yourself. Super Can-do people with highly developed or emerging Seventh Senses never give up that option nor forget the possibility that your time and your location can just be against you and you may have to do something totally out of the box. You can move. You can choose a different location but you can't choose the time in which you live. Just knowing this one fact could probably save millions of lives each year. If all of the people in the world that are totally desperate and devoid of hope would just get this one point maybe they could have a future. That's right.

Think of those people who have lost just about everything and who find themselves on the verge of suicide because they see no way out. If they would just consider taking the geographical cure many times their problems could be solved. Now some of you who are friends of Bill W. will scoff at what I am referring to and say that the geographical cure is a myth and the traveler brings himself. I cannot and will not disagree with the second part of this premise. But if you have a shattered reputation and you can no longer make it in the town you currently live in, go someplace where they don't know you. Isn't that what the witness protection plan is all about? I am not saying it is a perfect solution but it gives individuals a second chance and a second chance is better than no chance.

Mega-ton Moment #13

Remember, if you don't like where you live, you can choose a different location but you can't choose the time in which you live. Maintaining a sense of time and place will help you make realistic decisions.

14

When You Start

As your Seventh Sense begins to speak to you, you gain insight and realize that "you <u>Can Do</u> everything, but **when you start is important**." If you haven't heard what I am about to tell you then let me say it again,

"There are two times to plant a tree, today and 20 years ago."

There is something truly miraculous that occurs when you plant a tree. As time goes by it grows and gets bigger and you see this incredible being (it really is like a being and you don't have to be a druid to get what I am talking about here) after about 20 years. It is God's proof of the wonder of things and one of the greatest blessings you will ever receive in his gift of "perspective." I have been blessed in my time to have planted well over a thousand trees across several states but let me tell you a story that will serve to make the initial point here. Back in the early 80's I had the good fortune to be the head of the block association and would later become president of a neighborhood called Boerum Hill; it was and is a really cool and trendy area in downtown Brooklyn NY. At that time it was an area in transition and was not really all that fashionable but it boasted really great housing stock, close proximity (to the F train) and access to lower Manhattan and it was where Angela Davis the famous militant and Black radical hailed from. Two of the streets in the neighborhood received a grant from the Brooklyn Botanical Gardens based on an improvement program and it was called M.A.G. I. C. This was an acronym for; making a garden is commitment). They would give us the trees and the support materials, we just had to plant them up and down each street and make sure that each of the plantings were taken care of in the weeks, *months, and years ahead.* Hey, they said it would take a commitment, didn't they? (And it did, both on the parts of the tenants and the home owners and in terms of the really long time factor involved.) It was a wonderful opportunity to take two otherwise blighted blocks and turn them into lovely tree lined streets. Now if you think it was easy getting everyone on board, I have to tell you it wasn't. There were meetings upon meetings, there were selections on which trees people like, which would survive the tough urban environment, how we could protect them from dogs peeing, street gangs marauding, etc. and some of the more bizarre objections would come up night after night. Let me give you an example of one of my favorites. One night, when I was going over the drawings and reviewing some of the illustrations of the trees, I heard a shrill woman's voice,

"I don't think this is a good idea at all."

"Why is that?" I responded, really wrestling with how it could possible not be.

"Well," she proceeded, "trees bring thieves."

I went into a momentary state of reverie trying to comprehend what she was saying. My mind seemed to have been totally short circuited as I tried to figure out what she was saying. How would the thieves hide behind these tiny 1 and half inch trees? How incompetent would the victims have to be to not see them hiding there, as the would-be assailants got themselves ready to pounce? It made no sense, so I asked the woman, and I made all attempts to be patient because clearly there had to be a perspective I was missing.

"How do you mean that? I am not sure I understand how it is that the thieves could hide behind the trees, is that what you are saying? These are really young trees?"

Well, she must have thought me the total idiot because she said.

"No, I don't mean that they hide behind the trees; it is just that as the neighborhood gets more attractive and as the trees grow, it will look like this area is more affluent. If it looks more affluent, richer people will move in and the houses will get better looking and seem more appealing. Heck, everybody knows that thieves don't want to mess around in a neighborhood where there is nothing worth stealing, that's all. They will come here because this is a place worth targeting."

I had to admit it; she was right. With the good comes the bad, but as progress would have it, more people thought it was a good idea than not and we planted a whole mess of trees. As you might imagine, 30 years later those are two of the nicest tree lined streets you will ever see. Before it was a ghetto and now it is delightful, at least from the perspective of the passersby and probably the people that live there. I am not sure but maybe even the thieves like it better now too.

And as important as "when" is in you decision making the "what" is also crucial. Let me tell you about my friend Grace. Sometimes I would refer to her as Grace the balloon lady because she was the owner of Great Lakes Balloon Company and she was the one that helped me become a Hot Air Balloon Ride aficionado. Many years ago for my 39th birthday I decided to take my first balloon ride. I gave it to myself as a birthday present since after repeated hinting no one seemed to be stepping up to the plate. I arrived in the late afternoon at the place where the scheduled lift off was to occur and met with Grace. She looked at me somewhat in disbelief but did her best not to make me feel like an idiot since I arrived in what looked like my best navy blue suit (having just left my office). She said, incredulously,

"You're not going like that, are you?"

"Why," I asked. "Am I underdressed?"

"Well no" she sputtered. "But well, ah, um, well, you don't understand"

It was clear that she was groping for words. So finally she blurted out,

"OK, let me explain this, there are two types of landings."

"Oh," I said, "what are they?"

"Well, there is what they call a hard landing; that's where when the balloon comes down the gondola comes crashing against the ground. Sometimes it overturns, and many times the wind can actually drag it along the ground, and there might be mud flying all over the place as a result and you can get pretty messy."

I looked at her and responded letting her know that I had been listening very intently,

"Wow, that doesn't sound very good, what was other kind of landing you were talking about?"

"Well," she said, "there's what they call the soft landing. That's where the balloon comes down very slowly and the gondola just comes to a gentle rest on the ground, and when you get out it is almost like getting off in an elevator."

"Hmmm," I said, as I gave the differences a lot of thought. She felt better for having explained the various landings pretty well too. I could tell.

Finally, I responded with, "I'll take the Soft Landing."

The moral of the story is you should always choose wisely when you are given the choice. You may not, as in the case above, always have all of the circumstances within your control. That being said, especially if you are wearing your best navy blue suit, make sure you really choose wisely.

By the way, I got the softest landing you could have ever hoped for and I am not sure that Grace didn't take special precautions to ensure that I did too. Hey she did ask, didn't she?

Mega-ton Moment #14

You Can Do everything, but when you start is important.

Choose wisely when you are given the choice.

15

The Biggest Mistake of All

The biggest mistake of all is to avoid situations in which you might make a mistake. Nobody likes to fail. Anyone that tells you that they do is a big fat liar. But here's the deal; if you want to be the person that achieves, if you want to see yourself in the winner's circle, you have to allow for failures. No one fails if they are continuing to try and are still in the game. Once you stop trying you have failed. It's as simple as that and as hard as that. Let me tell you about T'ai Chi.

One of the blessings I have received in my time on this earth is the gift of T'ai chi. For those of you that are not familiar with this wonderful art form we received from China, it is a martial art that is typified by those slow graceful movements. We usually see older people performing it in parks, from Beijing to Vancouver, from San Francisco to NYC, and on beaches everywhere. It looks almost like slow dance movements and they are usually performed in group settings. The truth is it is a martial art and all of those beautiful movements we see practitioners doing have martial applications. The posture of "Playing the lute" is so very subtle but when applied it can be used to disable an opponent or break an arm. As one would imagine and as anyone who has observed, rarely do most of those that practice T'ai Chi ever get to use the forms for martial purposes but they are there nevertheless, and inherent in the practice. No, quite to the contrary, most people who "do T'ai Chi" do it for the incredible health benefits that include, increased flexibility, enhanced circulation, a development of Chi (the life force) and a general amelioration of one's well being. Those are just the extras and as such I am one of the most avid promoters of the art. I have also taught it.

Many times my students would come to me and before they would become actively involved they would ask if I could recommend any good tapes or CD's. I would always answer in the affirmative but would go on to suggest that they didn't waste any of their time or their money buying them.

"Why," was always the response?

I would explain to them that here's what would happen. They would buy the tapes and they would watch the people on the tapes going through the various postures and what would happen is they would watch someone else doing T'ai Chi. **_They_** would not be doing T'ai Chi themselves and they would be deluding themselves into thinking that they were. There would be little or no benefit. They needed to go through the postures themselves. They needed to move their arms, develop the critical sense of rootedness where as the Taoist sages would tell them, they would learn to **_breathe through their heels_**. They needed to do the postures and not merely watch some else doing them. Here comes the tie down. In order for one to learn the art of T'ai Chi one has to physically do the postures and before one can learn to do them correctly one has to do them incorrectly. There is absolutely no escaping this reality or this basic premise. Everyone wants to do the postures correctly the first time and it is virtually impossible no matter how good a mimic one is or how good a student one is. You do the posture wrong and the teacher makes a slight modification and improves it. You do the posture better and the teacher works with the student and makes slightly more improvements and so on and so forth and the process never stops even after the teacher fades from the midst. At that point the student continues to polish and perfect the movements until they become seamless balanced and implement all of the principals of the art (i.e. balance, rootedness, harmony, erectness, etc.) If the student doesn't experience momentary failure there can never be any progress (ever). T'ai Chi thereby serves us well as an example of how all the challenges that need to be met by any of the people that I will embrace as becoming students who master their own Seventh Senses.

Mega-ton Moment #15

The biggest mistake of all is to avoid situations in which you might make a mistake. If you want to be the person that achieves, if you want to see yourself in the winner's circle, you have to allow for failures. No one fails if they are continuing to try and are still in the game. Once you stop trying you have failed

16

A Creative Attitude

A creative attitude is the fuel of progress and growth. We have mentioned this concept of creation, haven't we? Let me offer you another perspective on this. When I was attending classes at Daemen College on my way toward getting my Masters degree in Leadership and Organizational Change, we learned various and sundry creative problem solving techniques. One of them is a something called "Six Hat Thinking", which combined with the idea of parallel thinking which is associated with it, provides a means for groups to think together more effectively. It helps create a better plan and enhances the thinking processes in a much more detailed and cohesive way than one could normally do on their own. The method is attributed to Dr. Edward de Bono and is the subject of his book, *Six Thinking Hats.* It is one of the coolest and most effective methods I have ever used in an attempt to help me get things done. I would heartily recommend that you pick up a copy of this important work.

But just to give you the thumb nail idea, here is what the program is all about and how you can use it. Let's presume that there is no one way to look at any given situation. If there were six people in a room trying to solve a problem or come up with the best decision they might make based on the circumstances they were confronted with, each of them might make a different choice based on their own individual point of reference or their particular pre-dispositions. Based on this premise, let's assign them a different color hat. The colors would be, white, black, red, yellow, green and blue.

1. **The White Hat**: the person that wears the white hat lives in the world on numbers, statistics and data. There is no right or wrong here, there is only information. All decision making is based on the facts as interpreted through hard, cold, numbers. "The numbers don't lie," is the perennial mantra of the man in the white hat. There is a statistic at every turn, a trend chart on every table, and a host of figures on every dry erase board. When in doubt ask the man in the white hat and he will have the numbers to back up any argument.

2. **The Black Hat:** is frequently seen as the bad guy, the man wearing this hat is sometimes called Mr. Negative. In the old westerns, the guy in the black hat was always the villain. Quite to the contrary, here however, our black hated man is an extremely important player in the drama because he acts frequently like the goalie in hockey and keeps us in check or helps the group not get put in the position of having "one slipped passed them." But he is always negative. He always has the final word of what can and what will go wrong. He starts many sentences with things like, "OK, in the worst case scenario this could happen..." He can be invaluable in helping us confront some of the most brutal facts of our reality. Without him we could get into serious trouble, indeed.

3. **The Yellow Hat:** is the opposite of the black hat. (You might have thought the opposite should have been white but we know what he does already.) When you think of the man in the yellow hat think of a warm and *Sunny* disposition. Much like Pollyanna, no matter what happens we can always find a positive spin. You just can't rain on this ones parade. If you are languishing in the gutter, it's a small step up to the curb. You can't live without this guy just as you can't live without Mr. Black Hat. He is the Yin to the Yang, the up to the down, like night is to day. When we start analyzing and speculating what it is we need to do, you will love having this guy on your team.

4. **The Red Hat:** If you are wearing the red hat you live in the world of emotions. Now what's important about this hat and what we need to point out right now is using this point of reference; ***all emotions count.*** There are good emotions and bad emotions and they include but are not limited to: love and hate, happiness and sadness, courage and fear, misery and glee, security and insecurity, pride and shame. This is the guy that takes the emotional inventory. This is the one who gets to measure the emotional fallout that might occur or be inherent in any decision or that will potentially alter any course of action. He frequently will ask, ***"How are people going to feel*** about this if we do it that way?"** I suspect based on this description, many people will tell you that Richard Nixon was driven from office because whenever he spoke to them they immediately put their red hats on and said "this guy feels like a crook to me." The red hat man plays an extremely powerful role in our drama.

5. **The Green Hat: Mr. Creation.** Based on where I wanted to take you in this chapter, perhaps I should have started with him. There is a reason I didn't. It might be true that "in the beginning, God created the heavens and the earth," but we are not God and we really don't get to the creating part until we have spoken to some of the other fellows in Club Chapeau. But with Mr. Green Hat around not only are all things possible, his is the land of "we could do this and we could do that." To everything there is yet another purpose and there are an infinite number of possibilities. After you have sifted thorough all the numbers of Mr. White Hat, and discussed the emotional toll with Mr. Red, and considered the disastrous consequences that Mr. Black Hat has warned us of and delighted to the dance of Mr. Yellow, we get to speak to Mr. Green Hat who offers us one more possibility. With him everything like the song, truly, "grows and grows."

6. **The Blue Hat:** Without this guy we never have an end. The blue hatted man is frequently the CEO who has to make a decision and live with it, but only after carefully considering all the facts and impacts each option might present. He weighs the pros and cons, looks at the opportunities and the pitfalls, broaches the good, the bad and the ugly and brings the matter to a resolution. He has the complete picture. Without him there are only pieces to the puzzle.

We started this chapter out by saying that a creative attitude is the fuel of progress and growth. I believe it is and I know that if you take any issue you might be attempting to resolve through this six hat scenario you will come up with much more effective solutions and you will find that your creative attitude will grow as well. If you don't have the benefit of sitting with six different people who you will arbitrarily assign hats you can go through the exercise yourself. Truthfully though, I should tell you that this problem solving technique works better with different people since you have the benefit of the group mind working for you and brainstorming works best when you go to a BYOB function (where you bring your own brain). One reason for this is that when you randomly assign hats to people it gives them permission to speak in terms that they might not normally embrace. The person wearing the red hat might actually be thinking that if we decide to do something "this way" that it will really piss people off. In fact he might truly think that himself. In an effort not to offend anyone he might normally keep these thoughts and opinions to himself. When he is wearing the Red Hat he has permission to speak the mind of the all of the red hat people in the world. You can't get mad at him. It's the hat not him. It is extremely liberating and gets people to open up in ways that would not be possible otherwise.

So let's try to imagine how you might use this model. Let's take an easy case. You have decided you want to lose weight. Make sure you use the S.M.A.R.T goal technique as you go through the hats.

- Slipping into the white hat you might consider
- the exact number of pounds you would like to lose,
- the change in your hdl/ldl on your cholesterol levels,
- the number of inches you might lose on your waistline,
- the size of you clothing, etc. It's all about the numbers.

THE SEVENTH SENSE

Changing hats to black you start to think,

- this is never going to work,
- how many diet plans have you been on and they have never worked before,
- what if you can't get to the machines you need to use at the gym,
- how difficult it is going to be to eat out in restaurants if you have to stick to a specific regimen
- The restrictive nature of what you can't eat
- What if you get stuck in traffic jams when you are on your way to the gym
- You get the idea….

Then the yellow hat points out that although all of these things might be true,

- It isn't that hard to lose weight, not really. There are a bazillion different diets and they all work: there is Atkins, South Beach, Nutra-System, Jenny Craig

The red hat adds to this and says,

- Think of how happy you will be when you have lost the weight
- How cool it will be when people ask "are you losing weight?"
- How wonderful it will feel to buy new cloths
- How envious people will be to see you looking so wonderful

A CREATIVE ATTITUDE

The red hat will also add,

- How awful it will feel when you fail, after all everyone knows diets don't work
- What a pain it will be to have to go out and buy new cloths since nothing fits you anymore since all your cloths are too big
- And this goes on and on juxtaposing each emotional shift

The green hat sees all of the possibilities. For the ladies they might be considering:

- The places they will go when they are wearing that size 4 black dress
- The number of guys who will find them more attractive
- What it will be like to go shopping at all those upscale stores that only sell designer cloths (fat people can't shop there)
- How their sex life will improve since now they are so much more desirable
- The possibilities are endless on this one.

And then Mr. Blue hat puts all the pieces together and using the SMART goal program we alluded to before one is able to CREATE a really sound and effective game plan that will be much easier to stick to each day. Go and create boldly using this approach and you might find that as time goes by you will become increasingly more comfortable wearing the green hat on a regular basis.

THE SEVENTH SENSE

Mega-ton Moment #16

When you are having trouble making a decision, try on a different hat. By changing your perspective, you will gain insight into the different outcomes that can result. Stick with this technique and eventually your green hat will feel much more comfortable and your creative choices will be made with ease.

17

The Man with Confidence in Himself

The man with confidencce in himself gains the confidence of others. It's a pretty amazing thing how this works too. The flip side of the coin also has its ramifications. I was watching an episode in the mini-series "Band of Brothers", which was produced by Tom Hanks and Stephen Spielberg. If you haven't read the 1992 Stephen Ambrose book or caught this wonderfully executed story on HBO, it tells the tale of the men from "Easy Company." Please, just put it on your must see or must read list and be done with it. It's that important and I would consider this as an absolute part of your home work assignment if you really want to understand what it means when I try to convey to you the power of your Seventh Sense. The men from "Easy Company" of the 2nd Battalion, 506th Infantry Regiment were assigned to the 101st Airborne Division of the United States Army during WWII. They were gallant men indeed. But for all practical purposes they were mere boys. These guys were boys of 18-23. They were barely out of high school and some didn't need to shave. They were what most of us would still consider to be "kids." Yet they are shown starting out in Paratrooper school and basic training. They then go through what seems like forever as they "hurry up and wait" to be sent into battle and are stationed in England. We see their involvement during the landing invasion on the beaches of Normandy, and ultimately we watch them proudly carve their way through the rest of Europe. In the final episodes they are shown as they are getting ready to muster out and return home after Berlin is taken. For my money, it is one of the best things that has ever been shown on TV and it should be required viewing in every high school as a part of their history class and it should be a prerequisite for their graduation. It's pretty tough stuff, and much like the Hank's film "Saving Private Ryan", it is very raw in its depiction of the day to day trials of the combat soldier. There is no mincing of words. There is blood and guts everywhere. It is the raw and naked truth. It shows us why these men went on to make up what Tom Brokaw accurately and reverentially described as "the Greatest Generation." My own father (who served in the North Africa campaign) was a part of this generation and these men were giants to us not just because they were taller than us when we were little children but because there was a much more clearly defined perspective of duty and honor back then. There was an easier sense of confidence in who we were in our relationship to the rest of the world and what our responsibilities were to each other. Arguably, it can be said, that we have lost much of this confidence because there has been a steady erosion of who we think we are and what each of us thinks we can do as individuals. The term "band of brothers" comes from the **"St. Crispin's Day Speech."** It is a famous motivational speech from the play, delivered by Henry V (in act IV scene 3, in the play of the same name) before a battle. (It is so called because October 25th is the feast day of Saints Crispin and Crispinian.)

THE MAN WITH CONFIDENCE IN HIMSELF

"And Crispin Crispian shall ne'er go by,
From this day to the ending of the world,
But we in it shall be remembered-
We few, we happy few, we *band of brothers;*
For he to-day that sheds his blood with me
Shall be my brother…"

But let's get back to our story. In episode 7 which is appropriately entitled, "**The Breaking Point**", the men of Easy Company find themselves in a battle near Foy, Belgium, losing numerous men. In the episode, the actions of 1st Lt. Norman Dike, the Company's commander, are examined and questioned. He is eventually relieved by 1st Lt. Ronald Speirs, who becomes the Company's new leader. In the opening of the segment the narrator describes Lt. Dike and he assesses his qualities as a leader. He tells us that the essentials of leadership are not weighed in the leaders ability to make good decisions nor or they held against them for making bad decisions. He tells us, what made Lt. Dike ineffective (and really scary) was that "he didn't make any decisions." We know what happened to Hamlet because of this and that wasn't good either. The men of Easy Company are really nervous and feeling very much "up against it" because the very next day there is going to be a major assault and they don't want this guy leading them into battle. Their conversations are bordering on mutiny. That's how serious their concern is and it is not because these guys are cowards. Nothing could be further from the truth. These guys were hardened combat veterans, almost all of whom having been wounded at least once. One of the sergeants, knowing this, really sticks his neck out and confronts the Captain and tells him, "Meaning no disrespect, sir, but he's just not there. If we are forced to follow Lt. Dike into battle tomorrow, a lot of good men are going to get killed." The Captain has been informed. He explains that there is nothing he can do about it and based on the opinions of one soldier he is not going to relieve an officer of his command on the eve of a battle (even though he suspects what he is being told is accurate.) If you catch the episode you will see what happens for yourself. Suffice it to say the Sergeant was beyond prophetic and the Lt. has to be relieved during the battle with bullets flying everywhere. It is a disaster.

Lt. Dike lacked confidence in himself and clearly his men sensed it in his meandering tones. They heard it as his directions seemed to be littered with double talk. They saw it as he literally walked away from confrontational situations where decisions had to be made and his typical response was

"Carry on men; I am going to get support."

Men in combat need a leader. They rely on their confidence for their own strength. To this end, we have the great and legendary Spartan King Leonides who has almost become synonymous with inspiring confidence in the hearts of men. But it was the confidence he had in himself that enabled him to stand in front of just three hundred of his men and look down on essentially all of Asia at that now famous pass in Thermopylae. It was the confidence of knowing who he was, what he and his countrymen stood for, and what would be lost if they did not stand up and engage this limitless enemy. It wasn't a reluctant and false confidence either: simply put it is what we call courage. Where this kind of courage comes from is less important than the fact that people need to have it and they will gather round others who possess it. And in the case of our Band of Brothers, they will flee from those that do not. Having said this, when you can show that you have it, people will gather around you too. So how do you get it? Oddly enough it is not all that complicated. You simply focus on things that are important to you. When you do that you begin to become passionate. When you become passionate people begin to support you. Many will not (remember the Schmetterling factor) but in the early goings a few will, and then a few more, and before you know it you have a veritable landslide of people who are for you.

It isn't just men in combat that need to have confidence. Let's look at the simple task of losing weight. It isn't easy and many will initially scoff at your efforts to trim the fat. But if it is important to you, you will ignite in yourself that spark of confidence and declare to your colleagues and peers and anyone else who is around you, that you are gong to do this. Then you will set a plan for yourself, either with a diet and or an exercise regimen. Then others will begin to notice that you are looking a little trimmer and you will inspire them to lose a few pounds. Before you know it, everyone around seems to want to get into the act and you practically begin to have your own reality show. And it works like this regardless of what it is that you are trying to do or get done.

"If it is to be, it is up to me."

These 10 words have to become your mantra for all of those things that are important or to which you set your mind.

Positive attitudes create a chain reaction of positive thoughts. But the most important part of this postulate is what happens next. The move from the world of thoughts and become set into actions. It is when these actions take hold that the truly remarkable unfolds. Although, some of us admire men of valor, we all admire men of action. Conversely, we admonish and look with disdain on the talkers and the Walter Mittys of the world. We all know that Columbus talked a good yarn for sure. And he did so all over Europe until he found his backers in Spain. But what made him memorable was he was a man of action and he put his money where his mouth was when he set sail on multiple voyages, criss-crossing the Atlantic erroneously bringing the Indies that much closer to home. It is truly amazing but I do believe that when you act boldly choirs of angels will come to your side to help you. We saw it earlier we when spoke of Rudy Ruettiger. But whether it is angels, or courage or that thing we now refer to as confidence, if you have it, you are as good as the golden child in all things that you do. You will inspire others. Your Seventh Sense will help guide you and lead the way.

Mega-ton Moment #17

Maintain a positive attitude and you will create a chain of positive thoughts that will lead to positive actions and ultimately get you to your goal.

18

The Right Tools

When one taps into their Seventh Sense they quickly realize that; they <u>Can Do</u> everything, ***but having the right tools makes it easier.*** Conversely enough, the great Napoleon Hill once said,

"Do not wait; the time will never be 'just right'. Start where you stand, and work with whatever tools you may have at your command, and better tools will be found as you go along."

Remembering these words, one day, several years ago, I needed to do a chore around the house. Actually it was outside the house. There was a repair that I had to attend to along one of the privacy fences that bordered the property. I walked out to the fence and there was a nail sticking out that needed to get pounded in so I adjusted the nail and, you guessed it, I didn't have a hammer with me.

"No big deal," I thought to myself.

I considered walking back to the house and I said well it is just one nail and perhaps it was laziness or stupidity but I decided to simply pick up a rock that was lying nearby and I figured I would just drive the nail in with this most ancient of tools. Again, I thought to myself, hey it worked for the cavemen, didn't it?

"No big deal, right?"

Well as you can imagine. Not only did I make a mess out of the nail but I made a mess out of my hand and there was blood everywhere. What the hell was I thinking? It would have taken me all of about 60 seconds to have gone back to the house and gotten a hammer and have done the job right. But no, I was going to take a really dopey shortcut like so many of us elect to do and "voila" I wound up with an absolute travesty of a situation. There is certainly something to always be said for having the right tools for the right job. Come on, doesn't it make all the difference in the world? More problems seem to get created by people who refuse to get the right tools or pay for what they need to get the job done right. How many screw heads have been stripped? How many butter knives have been broken or lost by amateur fix up men (aka husbands everywhere) simply for lack of this faculty that allows them to declare that we are well out of our league? Men are stereotyped by women for their relentless refusal to stop and ask for directions when the right tool could have been as simple as having a map. Thank God the invention of the GPS will relieve them of this burden. But again it is a refusal to get or use the right tool. The right tool in this case could also have been merely being another person who might know the way better than they think they do themselves.

President Kennedy was reputed to have had one of the more brilliant minds of anyone who ever had the good fortune to sit in the oval office. The accomplishments of his tenure may fall under question but perhaps they have merely become overshadowed by his untimely and tragic demise. But one of the things that I think really sets him apart from the other commander-in-chief was his personal obsession with surrounding himself by what became known as the "best and the brightest." His brilliance allowed for even greater shining in that he wanted men not of equal stature to his own but ones that surpassed it. Perhaps the greatest tragedy of Kennedys reign was not his assassination back in 1963 but the fact that this incredible think tank that he assemble never really got to realized any thing near to its full potential. There is a line in one of favorite movies, **"A Bronx Tale,"** that "there is no greater tragedy than wasted talent." As such, the talented men he turned to included: Pierre Salinger his press secretary, Abraham Ribicoff (Health, Education and Welfare), Dean Rusk (Secretary of State), Luther Hodges (Secretary of Commerce) and of course, his younger brother Bobbie, who sat as the Attorney General. More times than not the right tools are nothing more than the right people. Carpenters and other craftsmen know the value of the right tools. For most of the more important greatest things you and I will set out upon, more times than not when you look to gather the right tools you too will really be looking for the right people. Tiger Woods, the greatest golf pro of his generation has a coach. The late tenor Luciano Pavarotti had a vocal coach up until he retired from the world stage of opera. When we read James C. Collins's **Good to Great,** much of the book talks about the importance of getting the right people on the bus. More importantly for him, however, is getting the wrong people off the bus and the right people in the right seats. It always comes down to assembling your team the right way. Many people and even some large sized companies forget this principal and wind up with bad hires and wonder why these tools don't perform as well as they should.

The value and the proper use of the right tools is always foremost in one's thinking as one begins to tap into the Seventh Sense. It would have to be since it is this sense that drives the individual toward constant improvement. One will simply not allow a mediocre performance to occur if having the right or better tool would have enhanced the outcome. It does become all about outcomes and effectiveness, doesn't it?

Mega-ton Moment #18

You <u>Can Do</u> everything, but having the right tools makes it easier. Do not allow for a mediocre performance when you have access to the right or better tools that will enhance the outcome.

19

The Seventh Sense Will Give you the EDG

There is so much written about the subject of goal setting. We have SMART Goals, planning strategies, **to do** lists and so much out there, that if you took all of the books and articles that deal with this subject and placed them end to end you could probably go to the moon and back. There are good systems, bad systems, empirical systems, and fly by the seat of your pants systems. So "without any further adieu," let me give you an easy, guaranteed to work, program that you are sure to love if you can do it for just 21 days. Why 21 days? Because that's the time it takes for you to develop a new habit. If you decide to do it, you will see for yourself how your Seventh Sense will give you the EDG. The EDG is an acronym for *Effortless Directional Growth.*

Suffice it to say that planning each day and then reviewing your results at the end of the day can be a critical step in getting what you want out of life! Having said that, why not devote time each day to first planning and then reviewing your day. The results will be stunning! Do both of the following exercises at the end of each day before you conclude your work day.

Ask the following question: Did I accomplish my top 3 priorities today?

1. _____ Yes/No
2. _____ Yes/No
3. _____ Yes/No

Then go on to ask yourself: What are my top 3 priorities that I need to accomplish tomorrow?

1. _____ Why?
2. _____ Why?
3. _____ Why?

It is really that easy. One might say; it's as easy as 1, 2, and 3. Give it a try. You will be delightfully surprised at how effective it will be for you. But you are probably asking why this will give you an EDG and what makes it so effortless?

We have looked at many things that go toward making the person with The Seventh Sense more effective than the one who doesn't. One of the big things is recognizing the limitations. One of the biggest limitations is the fact that we loose focus; that we become overwhelmed by what I call the constant static on our own creative airways. The exercise above brings the power of regularly focusing on not just what needs to get done but what one's priorities are. It forces one to recognize what they are today and tomorrow, to the exclusion of all others. Could it be any more Stockdalian? No, and that's the beauty of the system. Dealing with the mundane, the cyber-babble, the psychological trivia and the normal distractions of life takes tremendous effort. Understanding what's important, takes so much less effort, that by comparison, it is effortless. Once you understand this construct you will be so liberated that only having to deal with three things will help you deal with so much more and those extra things or tasks or events that you were hoping to achieve will all serve as bonuses.

Years ago I remember seeing a guy on a talk show who had mastered the ability to survive in society without having a job. He went on to share that his was a life totally free of all obligations and he was stress free. He had renounced all responsibilities and he had orchestrated a life that made him personally happy and he was eager to share what he had accomplished with the viewers. For him he had achieved societal nirvana. No one could tell him he had to be here or there at a certain time. No one could tell him when he could take a coffee break or a lunch break or when he had to show up or be in a certain place. He boasted how he "earned money" by panhandling and how different soup kitchens were better than others and how he could get a shower at this haven or that shelter. He explained how he was able to get pretty good clothing from the St. Vincent de Paul Society and how even in the coldest of nights he could get a clean place to sleep at the City Mission. He even shared how some of the people he knew actually made pretty hefty incomes living this life.

There was a Sherlock Holmes tale that closely paralleled this story. It was called "the Man with the Twisted Lip" first published in the December 1891 issue of the Strand Magazine. In that story Holmes encounters a man who gave up his career as a journalist to become a beggar because even in that day he realized he could make more money in this venture than he could plying his normal trade. In that tale, this nefarious fellow says:

"I painted my face, and to make myself as pitiable as possible I made a good scar and fixed one side of my lip in a twist by the aid of a small slip of flesh-coloured plaster. Then with a red head of hair, and an appropriate dress, I took, my station in the business part of the city, ostensibly as a match seller but really as a beggar. For seven hours I plied my trade, and when I returned home in the evening I found to my surprise that I received no less than 26.s 4d."

He later indicated that he averaged *two pounds* a day or *700 pounds* a year. The point in the Arthur Conan Doyle story was the protagonist was making a relatively handsome living indeed. And the point that the fellow on the talk show was making was similar; in that he did not have to have a regular job with the usual aggravations and that by carefully manipulating the system he had freed himself of the normal stresses that most of us face in our "quiet lives of desperation." But had he? There have been studies conducted and sting operations launched in several different major cities in an effort to determine how much a person who embarks on such a life can actually make. I recall one person in NYC who worked the 42nd street section of town by Grand Central Terminal. He was bold enough to be interviewed by Eye Witness News (with his identity concealed of course) and he claimed to be making a 6 figure income. Now mind you, this was in the mid 80's. His ploy was interesting and somewhat inventive and pandered to sympathetic travelers. Unlike the character in the Sherlock Holmes short story, he would dress in normal respectable business clothing and he would tell people who were on their way to the Port Authority that he had just been mugged and someone had taken his wallet and he only needed $8 to get home to his apartment in Weehawken NJ and that he would gladly send the money back to the hapless mark when he got home that evening (ostensibly offering to send them a check). So why do I tell you this?

It is not to instruct you on the machinations of an alternative life style but certainly if you like, you can in fact choose to do this. I would hope that you wouldn't because frankly I think it takes an incredible amount of your personal resources to effect the kinds of outcomes that these scoundrels have, and my question to you is, and to what end? There are a host of variables and some can get you either arrested or killed and again to what end? Would it not have made more sense to have made wiser more socially acceptable choices? I think so and I would like to think that most of my readers would agree. But I diverge a little here so let me get back to your desire to get the EDG. By focusing on just a few things you will find that you can do those things to the exclusion of other things that might be time wasters or even time robbers. Let me give you another way for you to implement this process.

One of the things that Real Estate Brokers/owners/managers have to do is build their sales forces. They have a simple word for it; they call it recruiting. Now they may have other things that they do, but the life blood of any Real Estate (or any other sales organization for that matter), is to recruit. Many times when I would find myself going around the country training people along these lines I would tell them they had to build their offices by:

- Recruiting
- Motivating
- Managing
- And maintaining a roster of performers…..

But it all started with RECRUITING. There was nothing in their office or business that couldn't be cured or improved if they attended to this. So to that end I would give them a simple acronym to place by their phone. It was WDIDTTRAA: What Did I Do Today to RECRUIT an Agent? Before they could leave to return to their primary residence each evening, they had to be able to answer that question. If they couldn't do that they had to stay and do something (i.e. make a phone call, send out a thank you for seeing me card, etc.). So by extension, you too can become exponentially more productive if you focus on that one thing that will make the difference in your life. If you are in sales put a note by your phone that says WDIDTMAST (What did I do to make a _SALE_ today?) If you are looking to lose weight you might say WEDIDT (What _Exercise_ Did I Do Today?) Remember how the character Curly in City Slickers said it comes down to one thing. Make it then the one thing every day and attend to it and see what happens in just one month. Using this approach insures that your Seventh Sense is alive and well since the core of its efficacy is dependent on focusing on individual tasks, one task at a time and addressing them on a regular as opposed to an intermittent basis. It is very much the same approach that financial planners use when they tell you to set aside a certain amount to invest or save on a regular basis and watch it grow over time. They always tell you how amazed you will be over time. The reason why is simple…it works.

Mega-ton Moment #19

One of the biggest limitations we face is loosing focus of what our immediate priorities are. By getting an EDG (Effortless, Directional Growth) and following the EDG exercise regularly, you will learn to focus on what needs to get done now, and how to prioritize your needs.

20

The Language of the Seventh Sense

Each of the senses has a certain rhetoric attached to it. When we consider the sense of *sight,* we might say things like,

- "The colors of the sunset on the horizon were glorious."

If one was speaking to ones sense of *touch,* one might say.

- "The sandpaper was so rough it really hurt my hands."

If we consider the sense of *smell,* we might say,

- "The aroma of linguini with clam sauce filled the air."

You get the idea. The Seventh Sense speaks to us just as well. When it flows we hear people saying things like:

- "So should I get back to you Tuesday morning or would Wednesday afternoon be better for you?"
- "What exactly does that mean, when you say…?"
- "When exactly did you want to have delivery?"

- "Why is that?"
- "How is that working for you?" (Dr. Phil became famous using this one.)
- "If we did it that way, what outcome would you expect?"
- "Who else is responsible (for making a decision to move forward on this project)?
- "Where should we meet next time?"
- "What will be the agenda, when we meet?"
- "Who else should I expect at that meeting?"
- "What should I prepare for our meeting so we stay on point"
- "What are you expecting as a result of our meeting?
- "What is the goal?

Notice anything? All of these sentences are set in the form of open ended questions. They are all designed to gather information and include the other person or party. They are all orchestrated in such a way that clarity is achieved. The Seventh Sense when it is deployed becomes like a heat seeking missile whose target is **clarity**. There can be no wishy washyness. Effective people can't stand this. Mutual mystification cannot occur. When one says "We need to do something about that *soon…*" their response is immediate. "What does that mean, soon? Soon next week, soon tomorrow, soon next month?" There is no apology. There is always a sense of directness since the goal is to have effective communication. Without it, one party or both is always left with a feeling of not knowing exactly what to do or what to expect. As a result, people with the Seventh Sense are sometimes seen as a little threatening or even rude because of their relentless pursuit of being direct. They are always respected, however, since they get things to happen in spite of circumstances. This is because <u>people make</u> circumstances and if you can get people to do what they need to do in a timely fashion, things tend to get done. What is really interesting is when two people meet who possess the Seventh Sense. What do you think happens? There is almost an immediate recognition of sameness. They may not know what is going on and they may not know the name for the phenomena we have been discussing, but on an unconscious level there is a bond. The added bonus is you can be assured things will definitely happen. Neither party will let the other "slip one past the goalie." Both parties hold each other accountable.

As you listen to conversations you will hear these kinds of phrases repeatedly. As you tune into them you will begin to make them a part of your normal dialogue and you will begin harnessing your own Seventh Sense. Just imitating some of the patterns will make you more effective and will increase your own sensitivity to your immediate linguistic environment.

Recently, I found myself working with a client who is extremely effective at what he does. He is the COO of a company that is rapidly growing and whose market share runs coast to coast. In a conversation I was having, he indicated that they were having a certain issue they were hoping to have resolved. The dialogue ran something like this:

Joe: "So we are hoping to have that done sometime next week."

Me: "What exactly were you hoping to have happen?"

Joe: "Have the position filled."

Me: "By when?"

Joe: "Next week."

Me: "When, next week?"

Joe: "Next Thursday."

Me: "What time next Thursday?"

Joe: "Good Catch… hopefully by Thursday before 10."

Notice the acknowledgement. He was actually happy I caught him in the process of trying to be vague. He appreciated it when he got caught. He did not resent it. He now becomes more effective at what he does. He will get it done and move on. That is what he gets paid to do: to make things happen.So start talking the talk and you will find yourself walking the walk with the same level of Seventh Sense assuredness like my client Joe.

Mega-ton Message #20

<u>People make</u> <u>circumstances</u>. Set specific deadlines and operate on a timetable and you will be more likely to get things done, then if you set vague deadlines with no specific time constraints.

21

So Now What...

Based on the creative problem solving exercise we learned in Chapter 10 (You remember: What, So What, Now What?); so what do we do we do now? Ok, the "what" is, we have learned about this thing we now know as the Seventh Sense. We have learned that there is this other thing called the "Schmetterling Factor" that people possessing the Seventh Sense seem to have an amazing ability to resist and overcome. It becomes a big "so what" if all we do at this point is put the book down and say "well that was interesting." If on the other hand we take this new found information and move to the "Now What" position we can begin to use it for the betterment of our lives and our business. But first we need to recognize it in others. How do we do that? Remember we said,

- They usually walk faster,
- They seem to be a little bit more in a hurry to get things done,
- They frequently have "to do" lists in their hands,
- They tend to have written goals,
- They seem to radiate a sense of urgency,

- They avoid vagueness in their conversations,
- They seem to want to put things on a specific timetable,
- They know where they are going or where they want to go,
- They take charge of situations,
- They rise within organizations because they are performance oriented,
- They anticipate actions that could positively or negatively affect their plans,
- They are people with a mission,
- They are people that most people seem to gravitate toward,
- They are natural born leaders

There are numerous other ways you can spot these "doers" around you in everyday life. So having said that what should we do about it?

Well observing and taking notice is the beginning. Moving beyond this, how can you emulate these behaviors? "Right actions are the seeds of right thoughts," aren't they? Since each of us possesses the Seventh Sense in some size and shape in one way or another, tapping into others Seventh Sense begins to build our own. We thereby begin to become more productive and that much more effective at what we do.

If you are looking to build a business, it becomes, as James Collins has said, important to "get the right people on the (your) bus." Look for these kinds of people at any level of hiring and you will have a much better chance of getting your company to the next level. I like to remind the clients I work with that they should "hire for attitude and train for aptitude." Clearly if you are looking to hire a brain surgeon, the guy has to have the skill sets to perform those very difficult and specific functions. The reality is though, that given the option of hiring one of two candidates (with the same abilities) wouldn't you hire the person with the more culturally acceptable attitude and a more clearly exposed Seventh Sense? Of course you would. The ability to do the job should be a simple "given." Regrettably, most companies hire solely on the basis of ability and they wonder why basic production levels aren't met, morale issues begin to emerge, and goals aren't being achieved. With your newly discovered sensitivity on how the Seventh Sense manifests itself, you can begin to address the underlying causes of what makes for success and effectiveness in general. So the "Now What" should become a threefold procedure:

- Observe
- Emulate
- Act

Through the committed application of this procedure you will find yourself becoming the person others notice as being rich with the Seventh Sense. In the last few pages of this book you will see, postulates and principals and concepts that will stoke you ability to fire up the Seventh Sense within you. Work with the program and take it seriously and you will be the person that others will naturally gravitate toward: The person that makes all the difference, if not in the world, then in the room.

Mega-ton Moment #21
By using the "Now What?" procedure and Observing, Emulating, Acting, you will find yourself becoming the person others notice as being rich with the Seventh Sense

Conclusion

Wow! After reading this and some of the other inclusions that follow, one might say,

"That was some pretty heady stuff. "

Perhaps you should consider this one last comment to help keep what you have learned in perspective. It is a brief passage on that thing I like to call call.........Inner Strength.

If you can start the day without caffeine or pep pills,
If you can be cheerful, ignoring aches and pains,
If you can resist complaining and boring people with your troubles,
If you can eat the same food everyday and be grateful for it,
If you can understand when loved ones are too busy to give you time,
If you can overlook when people take things out on you when, through no fault of yours, something goes wrong,
If you can take criticism and blame without resentment,
If you can face the world without lies and deceit,
If you can conquer tension without medical help,
If you can relax without liquor,

If you can sleep without the aid of drugs,
If you can do all these things,
Then you are probably the family dog.

Remember Beverly Sills? What was her nick name? If I would leave you with just one thought it would be this. Life is frequently challenging and the choices you will make are probably difficult. They can even be serious, and it is too easy to get weighted down by them. The greatest accomplishments are made by those of us who are best described as being light spirited. Jesus tells us that we should "pick up his burden for His burden is light." Was he telling us it was light as opposed to heavy or that it was light as opposed to dark? We all know and we have spoken about those truly blessed people that seemed to be able to light up a room when they enter. If nothing else being light spirited makes one more attractive as a person. Just as moths are attracted to the light, so too are most of the people that one encounters in this world. We all gravitate toward the light. You will even hear some adults tell you that they are still afraid of the dark. Walk in the light and not only will you stumble less but you will find an increasingly larger number of people will want to walk along side of you. Maybe the number doesn't change at all. Perhaps you just begin to take notice of them. The more supporters you gather on your way, the easier your load will become.

What was it Albert Einstein said as he was nearing the end of his days?

"Why was I so serious?"

There is little argument for the value of his contributions to science. And certainly this genius, who was one of the greatest minds of the 20th century will be the discussed in and out of universities for years to come. And yet regrettably, if he could have done it over, he would have done so with a greater spirit of light heartedness. Isn't it ironic that his life's work had to do with light and the bending of light and the speed at which it traveled and that when it was all over and done he once again turned himself toward a different aspect of the light. So find your light and walk in it. Keep your sense of humor always, because without it the choices you make are that much harder to achieve and the fruits you derive from them will be less sweet. A big part of mastering the power of the seventh sense is the ability to keep one's sense of humor in the proper balance. It lightens your load and quickens the steps of all those around you.

"Light is the most important person in the picture." ~ <u>Claude Monet</u>

WHEN ONE TAPS INTO THE POWER OF THE SEVENTH SENSE THEY KNOW

1. They **<u>CAN DO</u>** everything, but not all at once.
2. They **<u>CAN DO</u>** everything, if it's important enough for them to do.
3. They **<u>CAN DO</u>** everything, but they may not be the best at everything.
4. They **<u>CAN DO</u>** everything, but there will be limitations.
5. They **<u>CAN DO</u>** everything, but they will need help.
6. They **<u>Can Do</u>** everything, but where they are matters.
7. They **<u>Can Do</u>** everything, but when they start is important.
8. They **<u>Can Do</u>** everything, but having the right tools

makes it easier.

9. They <u>Can Do</u> everything, but a well crafted plan is invaluable.

10. They <u>Can Do</u> everything, but knowing why it is important is crucial for their success.

Those that possess the Seventh Sense in abundance have these principals embedded into their psyches. They are simply a part of the way they are. They are hard wired this way and it is how they think. If you want to become the most effective version of you that you can be, let it become the way you think as well.

KICKING YOUR SEVENTH SENSE INTO HIGH GEAR WITH:
THE 21 POWER POSTULATES

1. A positive thought is the seed of a positive result.

2. **If you don't like something, change it. If you can't change it, change your attitude. Don't complain.**

3. The most significant change in a person's life is a change of attitude. Right attitudes produce right actions.

4. **If you really want to be happy, nobody can stop you.**

5. **Whether a glass if half-full or half-empty, depends on the attitude of the person looking at it.**

6. **There is a better way for everything. Find it.**

7. A positive attitude is not a destination. It is a way of life.

8. **The difference between a successful person and others is not a lack of knowledge, but rather a lack of will.**

9. The positive thinker sees the invisible, feels the intangible, and achieves the impossible.

10. The man with confidence in himself gains the confidence of others.

11. You will only go as far as you think you can go. The biggest mistake of all is to avoid situations in which you might make a mistake.
12. A positive attitude is like a magnet for positive results.
13. Our life is a reflection of our attitudes.
14. Positive attitudes create a chain reaction of positive thoughts.
15. Attitude, not aptitude, determines your altitude.
16. No man fails if he does his best.
17. Sooner or later, those who win are those who think they can.
18. Either I will find a way, or I will make one.
19. A creative attitude is the fuel of progress and growth.
20. Be the change you want to see in this world.
21. Forgive others and you will be forgiven.

These are powerful aphorisms. A daily commitment to meditating on each of them will help you capitalize on the latent energy that is your Seventh Sense. Make it a habit. It is not an accident that there are 21 postulates. It takes 21 days to instill a new habit or break an old one. Start at the top and work your way through the list taking one a day. Intone it to yourself or look yourself in the mirror first thin in the morning. Say it at least 10 times in a day, while you are driving, at lunch, before a snack. As you are dressing, etc. Over time it will become a tremendous source of power in your capacity to change the events and circumstances around you.

Each of us, who strive for "self actualization" which is what Abraham Maslow described as the highest level in the hierarchy of our personal needs, will most certainly embrace some kind of a personal philosophy. Many of you will be familiar with this now famous Pyramid which you probably learned in Psych 101. For those that have forgotten it, let me give you a brief explanation. Here's how one's "needs" run from the base to the apex;

1. At the very bottom, our physical needs must be met first. If that isn't happening all bets are off and you forget about ascending any higher. Those needs include: food, water, sleep, excretion, sex, breathing, and homeostasis.

2. Once our simplest of needs are met we look to maintain "safety and security" which includes: health, family, property, etc.

3. With these things achieved we can turn to love and belonging: feelings of intimacy, friendship, sexual intimacy.

4. As we near the summit of the pyramid we become concerned with areas of "esteem": confidence, achievement, respect of/by others, self-esteem.

5. And at the top of the pyramid we come to the world of "self actualization." Here, all of our basic needs have been met. We are now concerned with creativity, morality, acceptance of facts, lack of prejudice, problem solving and those things that lead us to spontaneity in general.

And as I make this point I should add that a book like this has little use for a person who is not at least making the attempt to ascend to the apex of this pyramid. I also think that unless you are functioning at the top of the pyramid your Seventh Sense will be function at levels well below optimum. So I will presume that the mere fact that this book is in your hands and these words are crossing the threshold of your sight line, you are included, and that you too are either creating such a philosophy or comfortable with your selection already. That philosophy or code of conduct, or thought process that makes you that thing that one recognizes as being a decision making being, can be as simple as an ingrained sense of fair play to as serious as what Stockdale found in Stoicism. As I have taken you through these series of chapters, with my postulates and my principles, it might make some sense; therefore, to at least offer you a final overview of what bought us to this point and complete the circle because truly our point of beginning brings us to this end. The following tract is from *Epictetus* and *the Discourses*

WHAT WE OUGHT TO HAVE READY IN DIFFICULT CIRCUMSTANCES...

"When you are going into any great personage, remember that another also from above sees what is going on, and that you ought to please Him rather than the other. He, then, who sees from above asks you: "In the schools what used you to say about exile and bonds and death and disgrace?" I used to say that they are things indifferent. "What then do you say of them now? Are they changed at all?" No. "Are you changed then?" No. "Tell me then what things are indifferent?" The things which are independent of the will. "Tell me, also, what follows from this." The things which are independent of the will are nothing to me. "Tell me also about the Good, what was your opinion?" A will such as we ought to have and also such a use of appearances. "And the end, what is it?" To follow Thee. "Do you say this now also?" I say the same now also.

Then go into the great personage boldly and remember these things; and you will see what a youth is who has studied these things when he is among men who have not studied them. I indeed imagine that you will have such thoughts as these: "Why do we make so great and so many preparations for nothing? Is this the thing which men name power? Is this the antechamber? This the men of the bedchamber? This the armed guards? Is it for this that I listened to so many discourses? All this is nothing: but I have been preparing myself for something great." (The Discourses, Chapter 30, Epictetus)

EPICTETUS (55–135 CE)

The following is a brief description and biography of Epictetus. There is a conspicuous omission from what follows in this version which is excerpted directly from the Encyclopedia of Philosophy. Speaking specifically to this point; he was born a slave and would later earn his freedom. This part of his story is of special interest to me because it parallels so many of our lives. I say this because, how many of us are or have become veritable slaves to our own predilections and self limiting beliefs? How many of us go through our lives with that debilitating "quiet desperation" and never think to give it another thought? It is almost as if to say,

"This is how it must be."

I think we have options and a realistic application of the Stoic philosophy and a serious use of our Seventh Sense can make the difference each of us has been hoping for right along.

"**Epictetus** (pronounced Epic-TEE-tus) was an exponent of Stoicism who flourished in the early second century C.E. about four hundred years after the Stoic school of Zeno of Citium was established in Athens. He lived and worked, first as a student in Rome, and then as a teacher with his own school in Nicopolis in Greece. Our knowledge of his philosophy and his method as a teacher comes to us via two works composed by his student Arrian, the **_Discourses_** and the **_Handbook._** Although Epictetus based his teaching on the works of the early Stoics (none of which survives) which dealt with the three branches of Stoic thought, logic, physics and ethics, the **_Discourses_** and the **_Handbook_** concentrate almost exclusively on ethics. The role of the Stoic teacher was to encourage his students to live the philosophic life, whose end was _eudaimonia_ ('happiness' or 'flourishing'), to be secured by living the life of reason, which – for Stoics – meant living virtuously and living 'according to nature'. The _eudaimonia_ ('happiness') of those who attain this ideal consists of _ataraxia_ (imperturbability), _apatheia_ (freedom from passion), _eupatheiai_ ('good feelings'), and an awareness of, and capacity to attain, what counts as living as a rational being should. The key to transforming oneself into the Stoic _sophos_ (wise person) is to learn what is 'in one's power', and this is 'the correct use of impressions' (_phantasiai_), which in outline involves not judging as good or bad anything that appears to one. For the only thing that is good is acting virtuously (that is, motivated by virtue), and the only thing that is bad is the opposite, acting viciously (that is, motivated by vice). Someone who seeks to make progress as a Stoic (a _prokoptôn_) understands that their power of rationality is a fragment of God whose material body – a sort of rarefied fiery air – blends with the whole of creation, intelligently forming and directing undifferentiated matter to make the world as we experience it. The task of the *prokoptôn*, therefore, is to 'live according to nature', which means (a) pursuing a course through life intelligently responding to one's own needs and duties as a sociable human being, but also (b) wholly accepting one's fate and the fate of the world as coming directly from the divine intelligence which makes the world the best that is possible."

(The Internet Encyclopedia of Philosophy)

ON EPICTETUS AND THE SEVENTH SENSE

Over the course of the millennia man has evolved. He has developed various technologies and in general at least according to historians improved himself as a species. I am not quite sure this is accurate. How many of has read or seen various programs on the Discovery Channel or considered the findings in National Geographic and the Smithsonian that seem to suggest to us that the ancients might have in fact known more than we do today. Various treatises that delve into some of the more arcane studies will describe the incredible abilities that our forefathers seemed to possess that are lost to us today. Some describe telepathic powers that the cave dwellers seemed to possess prior to the advent of the spoken word. Our more recent history talks of some of the unusual gifts that the Australian Aborigines seem to possess along these lines (which they now are losing since they have been absorbed into Western Society).

Incredible abilities to memorize entire tracts of drama and poetry seemed to have been commonplace years ago by average people and those abilities seem rare in this day and age. The

Koran, which was written back in the 7th century A.D., was originally recited (which is what the work actually means: the Recital). Truly few are up to this formidable task today. So the question is; "have we evolved or not?"

My contention is that we have not. The atrophying of the Seventh Sense in most of us will serve as one more piece of evidence for this position. The Seventh Sense as I have described it is so much a part of the Stoicism that emerged from the School of Philosophy that was authored by Epictetus (who was born a slave) and embraced by both the Emperors Marcus Aurelius and Hadrian. Were these then remarkable men? Were they? I suspect they were not all that remarkable in their essence or their abilities. They were, rather, remarkable in how they were able to take this faculty that I have suggested is not common today (but that was in former times) and use it to shape their own destinies. And this leads me to present the notion that this same faculty though dormant in most can be made manifest. The only thing that is necessary is the will.

The greatest need for our society today is the need for leaders. We need leaders at every level of our society not just in government but in corporate America. We need them not just in our schools but in our families. And to this end, the power of the Seventh Sense will help make this the best of all possible worlds to live; one the ancients would have been proud to have fathered.

SELECTED POSITION STATEMENTS MADE BY EPICTETUS

"Of all existing things some are in our power, and others are not in our power. In our power are thought, impulse,

will to get and will to avoid, and, in a word, everything which is our own doing. Things not in our power include the body, property, reputation, office, and, in a word, everything which is not our own doing. Things in our power are by nature free, unhindered, and untrammeled; things not in our power are weak, servile, subject to hindrance, dependent on others. Remember then that if you imagine that what is naturally slavish is free, and what is naturally another's is your own, you will be hampered, you will mourn, you will be put to confusion, you will blame gods and men; but if you think that only your own belongs to you, and that what is another's is indeed another's, no one will ever put compulsion or hindrance on you, you will blame none, you will accuse none, you will do nothing against your will, no one will harm you, you will have no enemy, for no harm can touch you."

Enchiridion, 1. Matheson translation

1. "Man is not disturbed by events themselves, but rather by the meaning he gives them."
2. "Do not seek to bring things to pass in accordance with your wishes, but wish for them as they are, and you will find them."
3. "It is impossible to begin to learn that which one thinks one already knows."
4. "People are not disturbed by things, but by the view they take of them.
5. First say to yourself what you would be; and then do what you have to do."

6. "Make the best use of what is in your power, and take the rest as it happens."
7. "Only the educated are free."
8. "Difficulties are things that show a person what they are."
9. "All philosophy lies in two words, sustain and abstain."
10. "All religions must be tolerated... for every man must get to heaven in his own way."
11. "Be careful to leave your sons well instructed rather than rich, for the hopes of the instructed are better than the wealth of the ignorant."
12. "Control thy passions lest they take vengeance on thee."
13. "First learn the meaning of what you say, and then speak."
14. "Freedom is the right to live as we wish."
15. "He is a wise man who does not grieve for the things which he has not, but rejoices for those which he has."
16. "If evil be spoken of you and it be true, correct yourself, if it be a lie, laugh at it."
17. "If one oversteps the bounds of moderation, the greatest pleasures cease to please."
18. "If thy brother wrongs thee, remember not so much his wrong-doing, but more than ever that he is thy brother."
19. "If you desire to be good, begin by believing that you are wicked."

And lastly,

20. "God has entrusted me with myself."

You know that your Seventh Sense is working if this last one hits a cord of familiarity with you. It is your personal mantra.

THE SEVENTH SENSE...

is that capacity to focus on what needs to happen immediately to get a task done and to stay on point. It is the ability to know intuitively what can be done and what cannot be done while still being able to place all limitations in their proper perspective so as not to mitigate an individual's personal resolve. It transcends courage, inspires both one's peers and subordinates and allows a person to withstand unusual amounts of ridicule while the process of getting the job done is being implemented through to its eventual completion. Succinctly put, it embraces guts and foresight. The person with the Seventh Sense is purpose driven at all times. With it the seemingly ordinary person is able to achieve what are considered to be extraordinary things. They become in themselves a force to be reckoned with and a person for whom to be dealt.

THE "SCHMETTERLING FACTOR"

The situation that occurs when people don't understand what you are trying to do or say. Frequently it will sound funny to them. As a result, you will be the subject of ridicule and overwhelming derision. This mockery may become so extreme that it might make one change or alter their plans, adjust their focus, modify their intent or simply forget about the whole thing.

References and Suggested Reading

- <u>Band of Brothers,</u> Steven E. Ambrose, Simon & Schuster New York 1992
- <u>The Count of Monte Cristo</u>, Alexander Dumas, 1844 Little, Brown, and Company, Boston 1889
- <u>The Discourses</u>, Epictetus, Classics-Unbound Edition 2009
- <u>Good to Great</u>, James C. Collins, Harper Collins Publishers, New York 2001
- "The Man with the Twisted Lip," Sir Arthur Conan Doyle, The Strand Magazine 1891
- <u>In Love and War,</u> Jim and Sybil Stockdale, Naval Institute Press 1990
- <u>Les Miserables</u>, Victor Hugo, 1862, Signet Classics Edition New York 1987
- <u>The Seven Habits of Highly Effective People</u>, Stephen Covey
- <u>Six Hat Thinking</u>, Dr. Edward De Bono
- Wikipedia, http://en.wikipedia.org
- Stanford Encyclopedia of Philosophy, http://plato.stanford.edu/entires/stoicism

About the Author

Author, speaker, actor, talk show host and 30 year business veteran, Brendan has been described as the "Patron Saint of Entrepreneurs." He has vast experience in developing people so that their full potential can be achieved. "That way everyone's bottom line is improved." His personal bottom line is often times summed up when he unabashedly tells his clients, "I get paid for results, (and frankly I get paid a lot, because I produce a lot.") His specialties include but are not limited to: marketing, product positioning, fiscal management, team building and rainmaking.

He is an authority on "Selling for Non-Selling Personnel" and a recognized expert in the Real Estate industry with over $1 Billion in life time brokerage and sales, and his book "Tricks of the Trade: a Real Estate Broker's Inside Advice into Buying and Selling a Home," (Adams, Media Corporation, 2004) is a must read for any savvy real estate investor. And he makes no apology when he is frequently heard breaking with tradition, speaking on such subjects that include but are not limited to: **"The Seventh Sense: the Key to Effectiveness in Life and Business,"** and **"Leadership in Jeopardy."**

Brendan is also a regular contributor with ezineArticles.com holding Expert Author status.

He is recognized as an Honored Member of the Cambridge Who's Who.

With over 1500 speaking engagements to his credit, throughout the US and Canada, this former Fortune 500 Business Consultant stands ready to get you and or your team to the next level. And with a coaching and consulting methodology described by some as one part, Dr Phil, two parts General Patton, a jigger of Colombo for color and a splash of Ellen DeGeneres thrown in for taste; he is guaranteed to produce results you never even dreamed were possible. He is a member of **the Coaches Exchange** and he is also currently the host of the weekly show "Getting the Edge in Business" on blogtalkradio.

Brendan, who logs just about more frequent flyer miles than anyone, makes his home in a Western New York golf course community just south of Buffalo with his wife Kathleen and a rambunctious Sheltie named, "Mr. Reilly". They have three grown children between them, each of whom are all very special and unique in their own right: Rachel, C.J. and Alice.

He holds a B.A. in Psychology/Sociology from S.U.N.Y at Stony Brook and a M.S. Certificate from Daemen College in Leadership and Organizational Change. He is a member of the Professional Business Coaches Alliance, and is a licensed Real Estate Broker in Massachusetts and New York. And although he continues to obsess over it, he still manages to play a pretty lousy round of golf.

Index

Excelleron Business Consulting: xiii,

F
"Fastest Gun in the West Syndrome"
Florida: 82,
Foreman, George: 49,
Fortune 500 Companies: xiv, 26,
Franklyn, Benjamin: 33,
Frederick, John: ix,
Freeman, Morgan: 17,
French Revolution: 92,

G
Ghandi: 79,
Gillespie, Gordy: 40
"Good to Great": 6, 80, 121,
Google: 4,
Grace: 98,
Grand Central Terminal, NYC: 126,
Great Depression: 69,
Great Lakes Balloon Company: 98,
Greatest Generation: 114,
Green Hat: 108,

H
Hadrian: 147,
Hamburg, NY: xiii
Hamlet: 115,
Hanks, Tom: 113, 114,
Hard work: 10, 11,
Harvey, Paul: 65,

HBO: 113,
Henry V: 114,
Hitler: 55,
Hoa Lo: 6,
Hodges, Luther; 121,
Hogan's Heroes: 36,
Holmes, Sherlock: 125, 126,
Holy Cross College: 39,

I
Iceberg: 9, 10,
Irish: 93,

J
Jeopardy: 17,
Jesus: 79,
Joliet catholic Academy: 40,
Jones, Tom: 93,
Julius II, Pope: 55,

K
Kovalsky, Dave: xi,
Kennedy, John: 3, 31, 120,
Kennedy, Robert, "Bobby": 121,
Knowledge: 9, 10,
Known Latent Defect: 87,
Kansas City Chiefs: 40,

L
Labrador retriever: 19,
LaCongo, Laura: 42,
La De Da: 43,

Trump, Donald: vii

V
Values: 9,
Vancouver: 101,

W
W, Bill: 13, 94,
Weehawken NJ: 126,
Welsh Coal Mines: 93,
White Hat: 106,
Will Power: 81,
Woods, Tiger: 18, 121,
"Windows on the West": 31,
Winters, Jonathon: 36,
Wright Brothers: 38,
www.WhoCanISue.com: 85, 88,

Y
Yacobucci, Mrs.: 86,
Yang: 107,
Yellow Hat: 107,
"Yin" 107,

CPSIA information can be obtained at www.ICGtesting.com
Printed in the USA
BVOW071951010513

319644BV00002B/178/P